Conflicts and Contradictions

Conflicts
≡ and ≡
Contradictions

Meron Benvenisti

Villard Books ‖ New York ‖ 1986

For my parents and their peers

All rights reserved under International and Pan-American Copyright
Conventions. Published in the United States by Villard Books, a division
of Random House, Inc., New York, and simultaneously in Canada by
Random House of Canada Limited, Toronto.

Library of Congress Cataloging in Publication Data
Benvenisti, Meron.
    Conflicts and contradictions.
    Includes index.
    1. Jewish-Arab relations. 2. Jerusalem—Politics
and government. 3. West Bank—Politics and government.
I. Title.
DS119.7.B3857   1986   956.94′05   85-40705
ISBN 0-394-53647-9

Grateful acknowledgment is made to John Boyd of The Lyric Theater,
Ridgeway Street, Belfast, for permission to reprint excerpts from his
poem "Visit to School," originally published in *Community Forum*, 1974.

Manufactured in the United States of America

9 8 7 6 5 4 3 2

First Edition
Designed by Ann Gold

Contents

Introduction

The most vivid memory of my early childhood is of a violent demonstration: a large crowd is gathered in front of the Jewish Agency building in Jerusalem; shouts of "Brits go home"; a British policeman with a sun helmet hits a man dressed in white on the head with a black rubber stick, and blood gushes from the man's nose and stains his white shirt. I was then five years old. We demonstrated against the White Paper of 1939, in which the British government stated its determination to keep us, Jews, as a permanent minority in the homeland.

Similar childhood memories of the heroic days are shared by a mere 3 percent of Israel's Jewish population today. Out of more than 3.5 million Israeli Jews, fewer than 80,000 were born in Israel before 1940 and are therefore old enough to remember the day the Jewish state was proclaimed: 37,800 of them are in their mid-forties, 36,000 in their fifties, 11,500 in their sixties, and 2,000 are in their seventies and eighties. Only one quarter of these sabras (natives) were born to a father who was a sabra himself.

This, then, is the actual size of the first generation of Israelis who, from birth, had bodily contact with the soil of the land, for whom it was a homeland, not a promised land—the First Generation of Redemption (Hador Harishon Legeula). We were the realization of the dream, the quantum leap from the ahistoric, abnormal, wretched existence in the Diaspora to a nation like all nations. We were to become the New Jews, healthy in body and soul, free and secure—unlike the weak, insecure Jew of the Galuth.

Our parents came to Palestine out of conviction, not driven by persecution or chance. They were determined to confirm through us their interpretation of Jewish history and their prescription for its redemption. Their ethos, and the educational structure they developed to sustain it, molded our perceptions and determined our cultural horizons. The ethos was so powerful, that half a million younger sabras born to parents who, unlike ours, were driven to these shores by persecution were also socialized to it and passed it along to their own children. Indeed, the Zionist ethos became the source of identity not only for the Jews of Israel, but also became an indispensable part of Jewish consciousness throughout the world, a dominant factor in the self-image of every Jew. The dream of a tiny minority of visionaries had not only transformed the land and molded the personality of their children, it transformed the consciousness of millions.

We, the authentic sabras, are today three in a hundred Israelis. Our minuscule number shocks us more than anybody else. Our inflated self-image as the rightful heirs to the founding fathers, and the admiration of many who depict us as the guardians of pioneering Israel, cause us to overestimate our numerical and specific weight. As a social group our story is less relevant to Israel's future than that of the children of the impoverished refugees who came after 1948. Their struggle to assert their place in society demands more attention than the disappearance of a dying elite. Yet one must examine the Zionist ethos in relation to the passing of time and changing circumstances. Indeed, one is unable to understand the denouement of the Zionist dream without following our tortuous path. For us it is a personal journey, not a case study in the history of ideas or an assumed identity.

In 1982 I was again mobilized. The war in Lebanon was my fourth war. This time my elder son joined me. We came to bid my parents farewell. Around the coffee table we counted the wars we share among us. My father fought for the liberation of Palestine from the Turks in 1917–18 under a British flag. He fought the Arabs in 1920, 1929, and 1936, and was wounded during his last war, in 1948. Then I took over: 1956, 1967, 1973, 1982. Now came my son's turn, and very soon my second son will be drafted. Almost a century of warfare was discussed and shared around a coffee table by three generations of an ordinary peace-loving family. My mother, a veteran Zionist pioneer herself, must have reflected on her dream of turning Israel into the only safe haven for the Jewish people. Yes, she believed in the just cause of our wars, and perceived them as wars for sheer survival. Yet even in her nightmares sixty years ago she did not dream that her grandsons would be unsafe in the haven she created. Her way of expressing disillusionment was the typical Jewish question-plea: *"Ma yihye hasof?"* ("What will be the end?"). Something has gone wrong.

When the hundred-year war enters its second century, questions raised cannot be dismissed as mere battle fatigue: What is our share in that endless cycle of bloodshed? Is it really predetermined by the Zionist program and is it still necessary to realize its objectives? Is it pre-programmed in our genes as Jews to be forever a nation apart? If our lives are bound to revolve around the next call-up, how can we possibly strive to attain other cherished goals, such as the creation of a better society? Are we entitled to make a choice —are we not compelled to formulate a new national agenda to replace the century-old Zionist program?

For many, these questions are sacrilege. The ethos is so overpowering, and the socialization to it so complete, that whoever dares to question basic precepts becomes a traitor. As Zionist ideology assumed a central role in Jewish identity, doubts about it amount to the negation of Jewish consciousness. Questions keep emerging but remain mute, expressed in the forms of alienation, emigration of young Israelis, the emergence of racist Jews, violence in society, the widening gap between Israel and the Diaspora, and a general feeling of inadequacy. The uneasiness signifies a growing gulf between ideology and reality. The sacrosanct ideology is never questioned, however. Confusion is attributed to weakness and loss of basic values. Therefore, the remedy prescribed is even larger doses of indoctrination. Even radical, leftist Zionist movements use a most orthodox slogan: return to the old values.

This orthodoxy is a typical attribute of the Zionist postrevolutionary phase. Our parents were successful revolutionaries; they broke with their past, its ethos and values. With their dedication and enormous willpower they created a new value system and novel social structures. They instilled in us their new revolutionary ethos but not their revolutionary zeal. We were indoctrinated to be loyal to the newly created ideology and to consolidate the new structure. Offspring of rebels must be tame and loyal, otherwise revolutions would not take root. We accepted our assigned passive role along with an active role in constructing the new edifice. The same loyalty to the ethos, with a high degree of technical competence, still characterizes us now, after our parents have passed away.

We remain loyal to our parents' ethos, but we inherited with it their internal contradictions. They rebelled against their past yet were firmly rooted in it. They created a new ethos but used building blocks quarried from the rich deposits of their spiritual heritage. The deep sense of historical continuity—"remember the days of old," the essence of Judaism—compelled them to perceive the Zionist revolution, one of the most radical in history, as a link in an unbroken chain. They were unable to perceive how radical it really had been. When some of them, on the eve of their lives, realized the full magnitude of their revolution, they were appalled.

This conservative-revolutionary polarity was for our parents a powerful source of energy, but also one of restraint. They were audacious but had a strong sense of proportion. We internalized their contradictions, but in us they caused ambivalence and confusion. We were told to repudiate their past yet to cherish it; to be natives of the land yet to regard it as a mystical entity; to dedicate ourselves to manual labor yet to finish university; to be professional warriors yet humanists; to be better Jews yet to identify with Diaspora Jews; to be secular yet traditional; to speak a new language that alienated us from world literature yet to maintain links with Western culture.

We accepted these inherent contradictions as a valid and coherent ideology, for we respected the legitimacy of our parents' internal struggle. We saw through their fiery rhetoric and beyond their public posture; we knew them intimately, at home. We heard them counting in their native tongues, Yiddish, Spanish, or Arabic; saw them reading Goethe or Pushkin in the original; suffering from the heat, and longing for the green forests and broad rivers; painfully adjusting to the ways of the Orient; going to synagogue on yahrzeit; oscillating between peace and belligerence, submission and defiance, flexibility and stubbornness, ethnocentrism and universalism. It all blended with the self-righteous, pompous, and radical public utterances into a multidimensional, human, and self-deceiving message. It was that same ethos that won the hearts and minds of millions of Jews around the world, inspiring in its audacity yet adhering to common Jewish and universal values, demanding diffused loyalty, political, moral, and financial support but not personal commitment.

We have internalized our parents' contradictions and thus established, through them, a link with the past, the same past that we have been told to repudiate. We have inherited, through our personal contact with them, the human dimensions of the Zionist ethos. Yet we find great difficulty in bequeathing it to our children. The unique blend of old and new, the unity of contradictions, indeed the self-deception that allowed it, could not survive them. It was subjective, part of their life story and experience, not part of ours. We grew up to face the reality created by their subjective will—the outcome of the Zionist revolution. The full extent of its success is manifested by the transformation from a dispersed minority to a powerful nation, from self-identification to compulsory affiliation by Jewish state laws, from persecution to oppression. The reconciliation of conflicting values became untenable. Forever loyal to our parents, we cling to the formal, declared ideology, but its human element is missing; it is flat, one-dimensional, and increasingly divorced from reality. We are unable to fully perceive that new reality because we are neither in the bondage of Egypt nor in the Promised Land; we are wanderers in the desert, a lost generation.

Our children, third-generation Israelis, are a robust and enterprising breed. They are free of our ambivalence and, unlike us, are not dwarfed by their parents. They are the true natives of the land. They will find their own answers and will mold their world in their own image. But unless an attempt is made to provide them with a sense of continuity, an irreversible break with the past will occur, and with it a permanent damage to Jewish self-identity. We can convey to them this message, for through our ambivalence we represent both the bond and the break.

My children, like myself before them, see through their parents' rhetoric and sense our tribulations. By sharing with them my contradictions, I wish to bequeath to them the human values I inherited from my parents. This is, therefore, a book about contradictions.

Conflicts and Contradictions

1

Internal Landscapes

I was born in Jerusalem. Since childhood I have
breathed its contrasts, physical and spiritual: the dynamic
confrontation of the desert and the sown, the mundane and
the eternal, the East and the West, the Jew and the Arab.
These opposites, threatening to tear the holy city apart, are
miraculously fused into a single unity. Since childhood I have
created an anthropomorphic image of my city. It is for me a
living, breathing entity. I sought to identify my inner contradictions with her contrasts. They captivate me. They go
deeper than my emotions, touch upon my most basic layers of
consciousness: who I am, where I come from, the people to
whom I belong. If my city is torn asunder and will never find
rest, then there is some cosmic meaning to my own tribulations, my own incongruities. As my city is composed of symbols and contrasts, so is my internal landscape. The
unresolved enigma of Jerusalem has taught me a great secret: answers are less important than questions. It is like
going on a tough hike through the desert. You are wearied by
the heat, you long to quench your thirst, and you press onward. But when you reach your oasis, the hike, the quest
itself is over.

I am not afraid of contradictions. It is like being in a powerful magnetic field. As long as you recognize it and are prepared to pay the price, you have in a certain manner come to
terms with yourself. My world consists of demons and angels,

3

symbols and contexts. I am not concerned with facts in themselves, but in the way in which these facts integrate into
broader frameworks. I am obsessed with conflicts, yet I am
aware at the same time that many conflicts may be insoluble.
I am not looking for answers; I am looking for questions.
People are generally only prepared to define a problem if they
have a solution for it; then it is manageable. I tend to go
beyond the problems to the conditions that created them.
Conditions have no solutions. They are insoluble givens.

If you accept the fact that the world is composed of opposites, of legitimate contradictions, claims, and counterclaims,
and that if one claim is satisfied, others will remain un-
satisfied, then in a sense you solve nothing. But you do learn
an important lesson: how to differentiate between understanding and acceptance. Recognizing the legitimacy of conflicting claims allows one to understand the nature of conflicts
without passing judgment. Acceptance or rejection of counterclaims, unlike understanding, requires a choice, or value
judgment. Few conflicts involve absolute truths; most are
between legitimate positions containing relative truths. And
it is hard to make a choice while acknowledging relative
truths. That is why understanding is avoided and confused
with acceptance. Yet conflicts are more often resolved by the
reconciliation of legitimate claims than by the making of
value judgments. Therefore, exposure to contrasts constitutes a first step toward a solution.

All this is elementary, but, alas, not in my environment. My
city nurtures absolute truths; my people believe that their
struggle involves absolute justice and so do my neighbors and
enemies, the Palestinians. I see everywhere the contrasts, the
incongruities, and they reinforce my internal landscape. Consequently I cannot live harmoniously with myself and with
my environment. I suffer from an almost permanent sense of
dissonance.

I live in a small stone house on the slope of the valley of
Hinnom, the traditional Hell's Gate. Across the valley I see

Mount Moriah, the one place on earth where man stands in the presence of godliness. Across the valley two founders of great religions ascended to heaven. The slopes are covered by a multitude of tombstones. The tomb of Absalom, of the Virgin Mary, Catholic cemeteries, Muslim cemeteries, and the cemetery of my own people on the Mount of Olives. Just below Dominus Flevit, where Jesus sat and wept over the destruction of the Temple, lies the place where I shall be buried, among my ancestors, in the old Sephardic section. Sitting on the balcony with my children in clear view of our place of eternal rest, I cannot escape the profoundest mystery of all.

Across the valley, to the west, I see the towers of downtown Jerusalem. The squat, massive silhouette of the King David Hotel dominates the skyline.

My house is poised on the very edge of the wilderness of Judah and the evergreen Mediterranean hills. The contrast between the gray-white barren slopes of the wilderness and across the watershed—the brown and dark green hillside—marks the dramatic transition from one ecosystem to another. The sharp relief of the deep canyons descending steeply to the steel-blue sheet of the Dead Sea assumes a masculine, almost brutal quality. The round hills and gentle slopes to the west, in contrast, are feminine, erotic.

Consider the clash of opposites between the settled country and the wilderness. One cannot understand the history of the Jewish people without realizing that essentially we are desert people. In the desert there is nothing you can attach to. There may be massive rock formations, but what you are principally aware of are heaven and earth. And so in the most natural way you come within reach of perceiving the Absolute. You begin to grasp the phenomena that lie beyond physical things. And it seems so clear how we—the people and the religion—arrived at the belief in one God.

No wonder that in our communal memory our wanderings are preserved in all their pristine, formative power. "I remember thee, the kindness of thy youth, the love of thine espousals, when thou wentest after me in the wilderness, in a land that was not sown," says the prophet.

But at the same time we were drawn to the settled country. Moses could do no more than look toward the land from Mount Nebo. But the Children of Israel crossed the Jordan, settled in a land of springs, brooks and trees, and began to till the soil. Yet from the beginning we had to do battle to preserve our desert revelation in all its purity, to fight the cult of Baal, worshipped under every green tree; the deities of fertility; the death and resurrection of Tammuz, corresponding to the changing seasons of the sown land: "And I brought you into a plentiful country, to eat the fruit thereof and the goodness thereof: but when ye entered, ye defiled my land, and made my heritage an abomination."

No wonder that these words were uttered by Jeremiah, a man who dwelt in Anathoth, on the desert threshold, inspired by the contrasts of the desert and the sown. No wonder that when the devil wanted to tempt Jesus, he "taketh him up into an exceeding high mountain" overlooking the lush oasis of Jericho. Jesus stayed forty days on a bare cliff in the wilderness above the orchards of Jericho and withstood the temptation.

The proximity of the desert to Jerusalem is a clue to her tragic history. Jerusalem is the threshold of the sown, coveted by desert nomads. Holy men could meditate in their caves, perceiving the Absolute, and within two or three hours could present themselves at the Temple and preach against the corruption caused by the soft life in the settled country. It is easy to see how the proximity of the desert could nurture fanaticism and exclusive possessiveness.

The desert captivated me in my youth. I would stay in the Negev desert for days at a time, guiding youth groups. I used to immerse myself in the desolate landscape, study, observe, move about. In my search I discovered that my notion of a sharp borderline dividing the desert and the sown was inaccurate. The desert is not only a physical phenomenon; it is also a human phenomenon. The ancient Nabatean cities in the heart of the desert—with their palaces, churches, and huge cisterns—are silent testimony to the capacity of man to reclaim the desert, to extend the borders of the sown deep into the desolate landscape. Every time I visit Beersheba, it seems a miracle to me. Each time I see the University of the Negev in that thriving city I understand that all dichotomies are merely attempts to force reality into abstract models, to compartmentalize the world. You gain order but lose the texture. At a certain point in my life, quite early on, I grew weary of my romance with the desert and turned with relief—perhaps like the Children of Israel—into a son of the settled country. Now the desert appears to me sterile, empty. But like all great loves it left a permanent mark on my internal landscape. I feel how the observation of the contrast between the desert and the sown has been relevant to my other role, that of a participant.

Quite early after the 1967 war the Israeli government began retaliating to terrorist incidents by blowing up the houses of captured terrorists and their collaborators. In the eyes of the Arabs, the destruction of a house assumes almost cataclysmic proportions. The Arab curse *"Yahrbetaq"* ("May your house be destroyed") is one of the strongest they can use. They attach a great, almost mystical value to their homes and land. Their house and garden is not a piece of real estate to be bought and sold. This is their acquired corner in the sown, a sign that they have become sedentary, that they are no longer sons of the desert, that they have no use for the tent. Their desert tradition is, however, still fresh in their memory. They still call upon Bedouin elders to judge in matters of family honor; they keep their old tribal affiliation. After all, they settled only thirteen hundred years ago, and the contrast between the desert and the sown is alive. We who made that transition eighteen hundred years before them, three millennia ago, have lost our desert tradition. It is enshrined in our holy books but has lost its inner, immediate meaning. We buy and sell our homes. We live in high-rises.

We can order demolition of houses. We expropriate land and offer pecuniary compensation for it. Just after the 1967 war the authorities launched a vast afforestation program. Worshipping the cult of green, they planted the desert threshold with pine trees. The builders of the new Hebrew University campus on Mount Scopus covered the gray slopes overlooking the Old City with rich brown soil, planted it, and installed huge sprinklers to irrigate the green lawns.

The natural landscape is changing, and with it the internal landscape of the city. It is tortured, twisted. Very soon the wilderness will be covered with habitation all the way from Bethany to the Inn of the Good Samaritan, from Anathoth to the Mount of Temptation, from Jerusalem to Jericho. In the Second Coming, Jesus will not be able to distinguish between wilderness and oasis. Who won, the angels or the demons?

My father taught me the desert, and his Bedouin friend Hajj 'Abdallah al-'Ayan al-Ta'amri taught him. This is proper. After all, my own ancestors forgot the desert when the Romans expelled them beyond the seas. This was their first expulsion; there were more to come. Hajj 'Abdallah replaced them in the desert, and when my father returned, the Hajj was generous or naïve enough to reeducate my father. They were devoted to one another and always showed each other the greatest concern. But I have my doubts if we as a group have reciprocated. One day I visited Elias Freij, the mayor of Bethlehem, a place also situated on the desert threshold. A delegation of Ta'amrah Bedouins came and complained about Israeli land seizure and confiscation of sheep. I remembered then the first time I met my father's friend. I was nine years old, in the fourth grade. One morning the door of my classroom opened, and there stood my father, the headmaster of my school. With him was a distinguished-looking Bedouin sheikh. To my embarrassment, the sheikh embraced me in front of the whole class. My classmates mocked me for weeks: a Jewish kid embraced by an Arab? Very funny. Had Hajj 'Abdallah been alive now, he would have come to me to complain about the sheep, I thought. We were both helpless in that moment, the mayor and I. But it is too early in the story to insert this element that threatens to tear my internal landscape apart. I shall start with the thing that is closest to me: my family.

My mother was born in Lithuania; my father, in Thessaloniki. My mother came in 1925; my father, in 1913. They met in Jerusalem. So I am a half-caste, a Sephardi-Ashkenazi. I absorbed both of the great cultures they brought with them. When, however, I try to pin down my own personal identity, Sephardic or Ashkenazic, it seems to go together with my surname, maybe because my father always expressed his own heritage so emphatically. I think my mother's heritage was secondary in the family, not because she possessed no tradition—she comes from a family with well-developed Ashkenazic tradition—but because my father's preoccupation with Sephardic tradition, his insistence, at least in my formative years, that I should go with him to his synagogue where the old Spanish liturgy and the medieval customs were preserved, caused me to identify primarily with that particular branch of culture. What attracted me also is the sense of belonging, of being indigenous to these shores.

When my father came to Jerusalem he was fifteen years old. His father brought him here to study. It was not aliyah (immigration to the Holy Land) in the usual sense; we have had relatives in Jerusalem since the sixteenth century. Once, when I was in office as deputy mayor, I fought Jewish religious zealots over the closure of a road leading to an Arab village, paved by the Jordanians over Jewish graves. I claimed that the road should remain open and that if graves were found, they should be relocated because we should cater to the needs of the living. When I went to inspect the site I stumbled upon an overturned ancient Jewish headstone. On it my own name, Benvenisti, was inscribed.

We have kept family records since the end of the eleventh century, and when I try to sum up those thousand years I feel proud that we never left the shores of the Mediterranean. Of those years, we spent half in Spain and half in Macedonia. I like to feel that I am a Levantine. I identify with the Mediterranean tradition, in itself a tradition of contrasts—eclectic if you want, but basically a melting pot of cultures, a magnificent kaleidoscope, ever changing, but each splinter preserving its own hue. I feel at home in Spain and in Greece almost as much as I feel at home in Israel. When I went to Spain for the first time my father said to me in a very somber tone, "Had your grandfather been alive he would never have allowed you to visit Spain." "Why?" I asked. "Because when they expelled us in 1492 we took an oath that we should never again set foot in that country." "But that was five hundred years ago," I protested. "That's irrelevant," said my father. "As we recite at the Passover seder: 'In every generation everyone is obliged to regard himself as though he himself had actually gone forth from Egypt.' "

This is the essence of being Jewish: personal participation in the experience of one's ancestors. It is *we*, not *they*, who embarked on galleys from the shores of Andalusia in August, 1492 and never looked back.

On June 7, 1967, I came to take my father to the Western Wall. He looked at me with disbelief when I told him where we were going. The news about the capture of the Old City had not been broadcast yet. He stood there with the Sephardic chief rabbi, motionless. He felt as all of us did, that we were joining hands with our ancestors.

In Spain I went to Toledo and sat on the benches of Santa Maria la Blanca, the Jewish synagogue turned into a church, our ancestral place of worship; then I followed the steps of my ancestors to Granada, to Italy, to Corfu, and to Greece. I listened avidly to the stories of past grandeur: "One of our ancestors served in the court of one of the Catholic kings, Alfonso or Pedro. The king liked him and thought he was most knowledgeable. One day as they were walking in the gardens the king asked about the name of a plant. '*Bienva*,' said our ancestor. When they returned, the king wanted to display his knowledge to his courtiers, and he repeated the name of the plant. One of our ancestor's enemies laughed and said, 'Who told you that? The true name of that plant is *malva.*' The king, abashed, ordered my ancestor to be dismissed from court. 'Let me explain,' replied our ancestor. 'I know that the name is *malva* [he who comes in evil], but I could not curse you, so I said *bienva* [he who comes in goodness].' The king, satisfied, said, 'From now on your name will be Bienveniste.' "

In the Jewish-Spanish tradition, there is an important key word, *grandesa* (pride). One of my father's habitual expressions is "Improper": one should not betray emotions in public. Perhaps it is because the tradition itself is so sentimental that expressing emotions openly is frowned upon. A few years ago an article published in one of the militant Sephardic journals claimed to demonstrate how Ashkenazim had seized control, obliterated Sephardic culture, and with their Eastern European aggressiveness had usurped the state from the Sephardim. My father's attitude was that the article was scandalous not because the author was not in the right, but because to pour out one's feelings exposes one's vulnerability and injured pride, something that *grandesa* does not permit.

But this is only half of my upbringing. The other half is equally sentimental but quite open about it, in the great tradition of the Slavs among whom my mother's ancestors lived for so long. Russian culture is so deeply ingrained in my mother that it was easy for me to identify as well with the cultural influence that dominated and still dominates Israel: the Eastern European heritage. Although all our founding fathers are gone, their culture is preserved in politics, in the arts, in the national ethos. So much so, that Jewish heritage has been identified with the Yiddish culture of the Pale of Settlement. I remember my father's outrage when the late Golda Meir once said, "We must teach every Jewish child Yiddish, the language of the Jewish people in the Diaspora." Socialist ideals were molded along the lines of Russian revolutionary ideals; our political parties were founded in Warsaw; Shakespeare's *Hamlet* was translated into Hebrew from the Russian version. When we want to pour out our feelings we sing Russian songs and play the harmonica. Our education began with the "negation of the Diaspora": from a deep sense of shame and rejection of the wretched life of our ancestors in the shtetl before the Holocaust. (Today there is a counter-tendency: to instill pride and esteem for the glories and achievements of the great Jewries of the past.)

My mother sang me neither Spanish romances nor Yiddish songs. Between themselves my parents used to speak French if they did not want us to understand. Only when my aunts, my mother's sisters, came to visit would she cook sweet, eastern European dishes. I have aunts who are called Donna, Lucia, Luna, Señora. And on the other side of the family there are Gitta, Frieda, Sonya. These two different tribes mourn their dead on the same day—Holocaust Day. My uncles on my father's side were burned in the crematoria of Auschwitz, with the entire Jewish community of Thessaloniki. My uncle on my mother's side was burned in a synagogue in Bialystok. It reminds us that Ashkenazic-Sephardic differences are, ulti-mately, meaningless.

When a person like myself seeks an outlet for expressing his feelings but grows up in a culture that forbids their ex-pression, the result is that the contradictions are internalized. These contradictions brought me to the realization that I was capable of differentiating between the emotion and the means of expressing it, and appreciating the difference between un-derstanding and acquiescence. This realization has guided me in my writing and thinking. It has resulted in the fact that the sphere I work in today—and have worked in for the last eighteen years—is contradictions, human conflicts, not neces-sarily on the political level, but on the ordinary, day-to-day level.

I don't know how I was drawn to it, but I live with my family among Palestinian Arabs. There is no place you can better sense the gulf, the human and personal contradictions, the communal conflicts that divide this city of ours—indeed the whole country—than you can in Abu Tor, that microcosm that is our neighborhood in Jerusalem.

The human and personal expressions of this gulf, the way we're forced to contend each day with the deepest possible ambivalence, are going on just over the fence. If, say, we build a sukkah in the garden, we don't invite the neighbors because we are afraid we would offend their sensibilities when we make a blessing over the wine. When one of their sons returns home from the hajj, the pilgrimage to Mecca, they do not invite us to the celebration because we wouldn't know the prescribed way to conduct ourselves and they want to spare us embarrassment. Once, when the son of one of our neighbors came home from jail where he'd been sent for terrorist activity, we were indirectly involved. We were not invited to his homecoming celebration, but his mother sent over one of the children with a cake for us, and later on my wife reciprocated with a cake of her own. What we experience so intensely is the contradiction between neighborly relations and the political divide.

There is a marked difference in our life-styles. There are no shared rest days, holidays, or leisure-time habits. The alienation is especially felt during holidays that have external symbolic expression, such as Yom Kippur, Independence Day, or the month of Ramadan. I know that displaying the Israeli flag on my balcony on the Fifth of Iyar offends my Palestinian neighbors, but I feel I must: it is, after all, my Independence Day. During Ramadan the whole neighborhood except us awakes at 3:00 A.M. A blind man accompanied by a drummer chants in the street calling the faithful to prepare their last meal before the fast.

The access I have to the Israeli political power structure causes my Arab neighbors to solicit intervention on their behalf. They often come to ask me to translate official letters that are typed in Hebrew only. Our attitudes to law enforcement agencies is very different. The Arabs traditionally regard any external authority with suspicion, but they especially resent the Israeli police. They prefer to settle their disputes among themselves. Jews who find themselves in dispute with their Arab neighbors are inclined to call the police and find a short-term solution. But by doing so they increase the alienation and find themselves involved in a deeper dispute. Sometimes situations become not only tense but physically dangerous. One day my neighbor called me urgently. While digging in his garden he found an unexploded mortar shell. It was a remnant of the 1967 war. My first impulse was to call the police and ask for a demolition expert. But on second thought I took a wooden board, carefully slid it under the shell, very slowly moved it across the fence, and put it in my own garden. Only then did I call the police. If I had called the police earlier, my neighbor's young sons would have been detained for questioning about the origin of the shell.

The windshield of our car was broken twice within a month. I attributed these acts of vandalism to political sabotage and decided to alert the security services. Then, after reconsideration, I decided to allow the local power structure to handle the matter. I approached the local elder and told him my problem. The acts of vandalism were never repeated.

In our neighborhood we live in a twilight world. Our world is divided, as during war, between "us" and "them," "theirs" and "ours." We belong to our respective communities and share with them the fierce conflict over what is perceived by each side as its respective inalienable right—control of the city. Our beloved city is for us—Israeli and Palestinian alike —the encapsulation of the one-hundred-year conflict over the Holy Land. That aspect of our life is brought home frequently when from our high hill we see clouds of smoke, hear shots and the sirens of ambulances rushing to the scene of a violent incident.

The bloody conflict penetrates the close circle of our quiet neighborhood and causes upheaval when the security forces conduct searches in the middle of the night and detain Arab youths for questioning. One day I realized that every house of our Arab neighbors has been searched on at least one occasion and every single youth over the age of eighteen has been detained at least once since we moved to the neighborhood fourteen years ago. Three of our Jewish neighbors lost their sons in the wars of 1967 and 1982, and one was killed in a bombed bus. Yet this is not the whole story. We are not soldiers manning the trench line, viewing the enemy through gunsights. We buy in the same grocery store, sign complaints in our respective languages to the municipality on garbage collection, exchange information on pesticides, and sip coffee in the afternoon, watching our children grow up from both sides of the fence. Even under the severe external tension caused by the continued conflict, life goes on. We are simultaneously enemies and neighbors. One inevitable consequence of war is the depersonification of the enemy. If you do not depersonify your adversary, you cannot shoot him. One cannot depersonify one's neighbor. As an Arab proverb says, a neighbor is closer than a distant relative. So, we are torn between our affinity to our respective communities and our kinship as human beings participating in the same life cycle. Some years ago a bomb exploded in the garden of the house down the road; another bomb was found by the Arab gardener before it went off. We, in our house, heard the explosion as did all the other neighbors. Three weeks later the security forces arrested the eldest son of our neighbor across the street. The boy pleaded guilty and was sentenced to eighteen years. The standard procedure at the time was to demolish the houses of terrorists. I was a member of an official committee that decided on such matters. I was also the "licensing authority" that had permitted the father to rebuild his house after it was destroyed during the 1967 war by a direct mortar hit. The house was not demolished, and a year later we were present with all our other neighbors at the wedding celebrations of the second son. The photograph of the elder son was prominently displayed. Had things turned out differently, it would have been his wedding. Had things turned out differently, my children could have been playing in the street opposite when his bomb went off.

My house, the origin of my family, my neighbors, the inner circle of my life arouse so many contradictory themes, accords, and dissonances. It is an appropriate background for a person seeking out contradictions in himself and in his surroundings. Yet I must seek broader causes to explain my incongruities and my political thinking. There must be more fundamental reasons for my cognitive dissonance.

2

An Image of a Homeland

MOLEDET

"Grandpa, grandpa!"
"Come here, grandchildren."
*"Tell us, grandpa—we heard on the radio that we have gone to
   defend our moledet. . . . What is moledet?"*
*And they fixed me with the inquisitive gaze of children, waiting
   for my answer.*
*"Moledet?" I whispered with awestruck soul, "It's every person
   and all the people. It's grandfather, grandmother, mother
   and father. And the grandchildren. And the neighbors. And
   the children. Young and old. All the people and every per-
   son.*
*Moledet is everything—It's made up of mountains and valleys,
   sights and sounds. . . .*
*All this is moledet. It's the quivering of leaves on the tree and
   the shining azure sea,*
The red rooftops, the silver of olive groves,
*The first dawn light touching the mountaintops and the spar-
   kling droplets of dew;*
The joyous sound of birdsong, the dancing rays of sunlight.
And the laughter of infants, lightsome and strong.
All that, all that is moledet."

(Poem, grade two; translation by Marcia Kretzmer)

17

Aunt Gitta died in her sleep in mid-July 1984 in her room in Kibbutz Ma'agan Michael. She was eighty-seven. Two days later we, her nieces and nephews, our cousin Yehudit and the tribe of Gitta's grandchildren and their children, other comrades from the kibbutz and some surviving peers of my aunt, gathered together in the small cemetery between the fishponds. The ceremony was intentionally nonreligious. My father chose to read, according to Sephardic tradition, from the Book of Proverbs: "Who can find a virtuous woman? for her price is far above rubies. . . . She considereth a field, and buyeth it: with the fruit of her hands she planteth a vineyard. She girdeth her loins with strength, and strengtheneth her arms. . . . She looketh well to the ways of her household. And eateth not the bread of idleness. . . . Many daughters have done virtuously, but thou excellest them all. . . ." And then he recited the Kaddish. A member of the kibbutz said short parting words.

Then suddenly, and totally out of character, my mother, Lea, aged eighty-three, the only surviving sister, began talking. "Gitta," she said, "when I saw you for the last time, a week ago, we talked about father and agreed that it is all because of him. He, Menachem Mendl Friedman, the *iluy* [genius] of Volozyn [a famous religious academy in Lithuania], insisted that we shall talk in Hebrew, even in the Diaspora. He, as a member of Hovevei Zion [The Lovers of Zion—the forerunners of the Zionist movement], bought over one hundred years ago the swamps of nearby Hadera. He sent Gila [their sister] here with her husband Eliezer, one of the first hydraulic engineers who participated in the reclamation of the swamps of Kabara [on which Kibbutz Ma'agan Michael is built]. Then we came: David, Zorach, Moshe, myself, and you, Gitta. When you insisted on joining us, your husband's family objected. They were Russian social revolutionaries, but you persevered. When Uri, your husband, was killed by an Arab bomb in Haifa, they said you were responsible; but then, they all died in Auschwitz, together with our brother Kopel. Now we bury you in the soil that our father bought, Eliezer reclaimed, and your daughter Yehudit and her children till. The circle is closed. I want that your great-grandchildren will understand all this and will continue." My mother, an old nurse, accustomed to comforting the infirm, not to delivering eulogies, stepped back.

Later she told me that it was all improvised; she just felt that as the last surviving member of that remarkable clan of pioneers, she must serve as their spokesman. When she was led away from the grave by one of Gitta's grandsons, I heard him saying, "But Doda [Aunt] Lea, we are only what we are," meaning, "Unlike you, we are just ordinary people."

On the way back to the kibbutz I looked to the east, to the hills of Mount Carmel, to Zikhron Yaakov, the old Jewish colony. There my father taught after he was "honorably discharged" from the 40th Regiment of the Royal Fusiliers, known also as "The First Judean," at the end of the First World War. In Zikhron Yaakov he helped organize the Haganah (defense) unit during the first Arab riots of 1920 and met the Friedmans, later to marry my mother, an unheard-of mixed—Sephardi-Ashkenazi—marriage. To the southeast I saw Pardess-Hannah, the colony where I spent months of carefree childhood vacations, where in my aunt's little house a group of Boy Scouts was formed to settle in Kibbutz Ma'agan Michael. How deep, I reflected, are my roots in this land; how multidimensional are my associations with *moledet*.

Moledet in Hebrew means, literally, "birthplace." Its meaning is similar to homeland, fatherland, or *patria*. Its meaning in the most profound sense, however, is almost untranslatable. In the school curriculum and in the army the subject is known also as *yedi'at haaretz*—"knowledge of the land." Those who coined that phrase were undoubtedly aware of the biblical meaning of *yedi'a*, an act of sexual possession: "And Adam knew Eve, his wife." *Yedi'at haaretz* features in the school curriculum and in army instruction courses as a subject in its own right, incorporating geography, geology, history, ethnology, botany—and all this is directed not simply to increasing knowledge but to nurturing a deep attachment to the country: "instilling youth with love of country" is the closest you can get to the Hebrew term describing the objective of the subject.

The obsessive search for rootedness, the need to turn the *geographia sacra* of the Diaspora into tangible reality, to make Eretz Israel a natural, not only a spiritual, homeland— to possess it through the senses by bodily contact with its soil, mountains, deserts, and streams—this is what lies at the heart of the tremendous educational enterprise properly regarded more as a cult than a subject. Generations of Israelis have worshipped *moledet* in hikes, prayed to it by watching birds, identifying flowers, locating nests of bald eagles, testing their dedication by deliberately refraining from drinking water in the desert for days. The Bible became a guidebook, taught by reference to the landscape, less for its humanistic and social message—and not at all for its divine authorship. There is nothing more romantic and at the same time more "establishment" than to be connected in some fashion with this cult. Its priests are the *madrichim*—guides and youth leaders. An extensive institutional network sustains *yedi'at haaretz:* research institutes, field schools, the Society for the Preservation of Nature in Israel (SPNI), the Jewish National Fund, youth movements, paramilitary units, the army.

No wonder that the sabras, native-born Israelis, turned the romance with the land into a subject par excellence of their literature. Our most distinguished writers devote whole chapters, with immense detail and a wealth of description, just to physical features of the landscape. The drama in many literary works is less human than natural, an obsession with the landscape almost to the exclusion of everything else.

It is impossible to comprehend the Israeli psyche without appreciating the profound impact of the cult of *moledet.* One must also appreciate the reason for it. The early settlers, like all immigrants, were alien to the new landscape. The contrast between their childhood environment—the green forests, broad rivers, steppes—and the arid, desolate, brown-gray sun-baked earth was devastating. It was a tragic encounter between people who believed they were returning home but felt the utmost alienation from the physical features of their home.

"O my land, my mother, why is your landscape so desolate and sad?" laments the poet Rachel. Our national poet, Chaim Nachman Bialik, never wrote a single poem describing his physical surroundings from the time he arrived in Palestine. Yet for him it was not terra incognita. His intimate knowledge of the land was culled from the Scriptures and rabbinic sources of ancient Palestine. While still living in Russia he wrote the most evocative poetic works on the landscapes of his dream-homeland. The magnificent description of the wilderness contained in Bialik's great epic, *The Scroll of Fire*, has never been surpassed in its sensitivity by a native-born Israeli writer.

The Kabbalists and Hassidim who followed their rabbis to the Holy Land were better equipped for the confrontation with the physical realities of the land; they could retreat into a world of learning, ascetic discipline, and spiritual experience. The secular pioneers had no choice but to struggle with an unyielding landscape. Out of that predicament came the perception that the new generation, the first to be born in the homeland, should spring naturally from its native soil, as the poet Saul Tchernichovsky wrote:

> *Man is but a small piece of land*
> *Man is but an image of his homeland's landscape.*

Yet the pioneers refused to abandon the mythic images of their *geographia sacra;* they wanted to fuse ancient symbols and reality so that the primary experience of contact with the soil would be enriched by the spiritual heritage. Thus *yedi'at haaretz* came into being encompassing the study of the land in all its aspects and the history of the Jewish people's attachment to it. *Moledet* became the pivot around which the entire Israeli educational system would revolve.

In trying to clarify this unique concept and educational

approach, I can do no better than to quote some of my father's writings from the thirties in which he extolled the virtue and benefits of *yedi'at haaretz*. For generations of young people my father's and his colleagues' names were synonymous with *moledet*. What gives these writings added piquancy is that he reissued them after the 1967 war with a preface explaining that those principles had acquired added relevancy "since parts of the homeland beyond our reach prior to the Six-Day War [the West Bank] have now been opened to us." In other words, the process of nurturing a deep attachment to the landscape was to be reapplied to the areas of Eretz Israel liberated in the 1967 war.

In a clear, rhythmic Hebrew prose, full of biblical and talmudic allusion, my father lists the various benefits flowing from the hiking experience: bodily fitness from the muscular effort and self-discipline, renewed vitality, joy from the cleansing experience of being in natural, unspoiled surroundings. "The bad habits born of pampering and laziness at home give way in the company of others to social solidarity, mutual aid, self-exertion, steadfastness, resilience, and maturity. Moments of adventure or even danger strengthen bonds of comradeship that will stand the test in time of war." Youth well versed in the topography of the country strengthen national defense. Nurturing attachment to different regions of the country will inspire hikers to return as settlers. Visiting different Jewish communities will cause the hiker to appreciate the full significance of the "ingathering of the exiles." "Hiking will endow the pupil with a better understanding of the Bible, Jewish history, Jewish heroism, and the life of our ancestors." This last point, ironically enough, is emphasized with respect to knowing the Arab community: ". . . to acquire an understanding of more ancient ways of life, going back to the days of the Patriarchs." Visiting Arabs is also considered important "to set our relationship with them on a correct and neighborly footing."

I am not sure that the kind of thing I am describing here exists in any other part of the world. It has, of course, a lot in common with the Scouting movement in the British Isles and summer camps in the United States. It certainly has many features in common with the German nature and rambling movements of the twenties that profoundly affected Zionist youth in Germany and central Europe. The German Zionist Blau-Weiss movement, founded in 1912, was based on the love of nature, unspoiled surroundings, and the development of self-reliant personalities, sound in mind and body. Closely associated with these aims was the idea of a cultural renaissance, and in other Jewish youth movements, socialist ideology as well. Here the critique of educated Jewish youth of the urbanized Jewish community with its "unhealthy, narrow cultural horizons" directly paralleled the critique of German gentile youth of philistinism, and the ills of modern civilization.

But *moledet* is more than a cultural and character-forming experience. It is a positive act, probably unique, of possessing the land. When you hike in the desert you actively possess its wadis and rocky promontories. The circuitous mountain roads skirting dense pine forests become Jewish when you drive along them. Sighting gazelles, identifying wild plants, excavating archaeological sites are all symbolic acts of possession. Caring about the homeland proves ownership. Cultivation is a more valid proof of ownership than a title deed. After all, who would make the effort to look after something that does not belong to him?

Immediately after the Six-Day War, in the newly conquered territories still littered with incinerated tanks and other detritus of war, the SPNI put up signs warning visitors not to harm the flora and fauna of the region. This seemed to many Israelis ample testimony that even with all the military and strategic considerations, someone had a sensitive and civilized concern for the environment. But this kind of sensitivity, the result of countless hours of *yedi'at haaretz,* served another purpose: the establishing of a claim. There is a corollary to this attitude: neglect of the ecology of the homeland by others is a sure sign that they have no right to the land. The test of possession is caring. One can find in *yedi'at ha-*

aretz literature ample references to Arab neglect of the land to the point of transforming cultivated regions into wilderness. A famous saying coined by a British governor of Sinai, Jarvis—"The Bedouin is not the son of the desert, but rather its father"—is frequently quoted. The vanishing of natural forests is attributed to the destructive grazing of Bedouin herds of black goats and burning of trees for charcoal. The erosion of topsoil that exposed the rocks and made hill slopes barren and uncultivable is attributed to Arab neglect of the ancient agricultural terraces built by our ancestors two thousand years ago. One of the most bizarre military orders issued by Israel in the West Bank was a prohibition of the picking of *za'atar*, a wild mountain herb, variously identified with thyme, wild marjoram, or hyssop. The Palestinians gather the herb, grinding it into a spice greatly prized in Arab cuisine. Strangely enough, *za'atar* has recently acquired added symbolic significance in Palestinian national consciousness since the battle of Tel-a-Za'atar with the Syrians in the Lebanese civil war. *Za'atar* is a protected plant because it faces extinction, and there is genuine concern for its ecological survival. But the military order banning the picking of *za'atar* is also a strong political and ideological statement: You Palestinians despoil the land indiscriminately because you do not feel for it, ergo it is not your homeland; we look after it, therefore it is ours.

Our sensitivity is to things. We are obsessed with the landscape, but the Palestinian Arabs who dwell in it are viewed in the *yedi'at haaretz* perspective as part of the natural features, a kind of fauna—objects, not subject. Arab villages and customs are a backdrop, part of the scenery. Their traditional, "picturesque" way of life is worth conserving as part of the environment, as a living testimony to the life of our forefathers, similar in a way to Indian reservations but genuine, not a mere tourist attraction.

When Israeli planners drew up their plans for huge dormitory communities around Jerusalem, their main features were fortresslike perimeters, high-density housing, and huge earth-moving activity that obliterated the natural relief. The same planners imposed severe restrictions on building activity in adjacent Arab villages so that the pastoral landscape would remain unspoiled. *Moledet* textbooks are full of romantic descriptions of the Arabs, their customs and folklore, always perceived as an integral part of the scenery though never as a legitimate entity in their own right, with their own national consciousness and aspirations. Many abandoned quaint Arab villages have been meticulously preserved with due attention to setting and scale. But they are empty of Arabs and are designated as "artists' colonies."

The SPNI was founded only in the mid-sixties. By then the whole landscape had been irrevocably transformed. Hundreds of settlements—cities, townships, and villages—had been built; millions of dunams (a dunam is about one-fourth acre) of orchards and pine forests had been planted; all the coastal rivers had dried to mere trickles, and the riverbeds had become open sewers for industrial wastes. The National Carrier pipes water to the Negev desert. The cult of development and the greening of the landscape—which sometimes stand in a contradictory relationship to each other—is the other aspect of *moledet. Yedi'at haaretz* is not a passive acceptance of the landscape but is rather a dynamic concept of molding it into a new form—modern, productive, progressive, and efficient. An indispensable part of *moledet* in the schools is agriculture; tilling the soil to create a primary and enduring bond with the land.

One of our most popular holidays is Tu-Bishvat (the fifteenth day of the month of Shvat)—"New Year of the Trees"—when children plant trees or shrubs in the soil of the homeland. An appropriate verse from Leviticus (19:23) made this ceremony, carried out on special school outings all over the country, almost a biblical commandment: "And when ye shall come into the land, and shall have planted all manner of trees . . ." The planting ceremony is the cornerstone of Jewish National Fund educational activity, organized by a "teachers' council for the JNF" that plans seminars and events and issues publications throughout the school year. The cult of green is an assiduously cultivated part of the national myth. National leaders and foreign dignitaries are taken to plant groves and forests named in their honor. A visit to a "plant-your-own-tree" center is an important event on tourist itineraries.

However, often in head-on collision with conservation and the greening of the landscape, construction of housing, industries, highways, and power stations has been carried out on a vast scale with little regard for ecology. The pressing needs of providing shelter for hundreds of thousands of immigrants and the creation of a viable economic infrastructure overshadowed all other considerations. The results are both awe-inspiring and disastrous. The most spectacular achievement is undoubtedly the transformation of large areas of the arid, desolate Negev into flourishing, productive, fertile regions. To realize that a generation ago the borderline of permanent habitation ran a mere thirty-five miles south of Tel Aviv is almost beyond belief. People who do not remember Beersheba before 1950 can have no conception of what kind of miracle has been wrought there. This tremendous enterprise of dozens of settlements, millions of dunams of irrigated cultivated land—a flourishing city with its own university and heavy industry—is an impressive act of physical creation, and also of strong emotional commitment to the Zionist vision. It has transformed this country dramatically, and much credit for the energy and motivation must be attributed to *moledet*.

At the same time, the cult of indiscriminate development has created many eyesores. The coastal plain with its congested bedroom communities, its polluting industrial estates, the smog, the unchecked suburban sprawl ever encroaching on the agricultural areas is sad testimony to the danger of going to extremes. Israeli developers were given an almost free hand, and this urban nightmare is the result. That it is barely two generations old, is almost beyond belief. It was only in the mid-sixties, when the devastating effects on the environment of this unchecked development became apparent, that the pendulum swung to conservation. But at that moment in time the 1967 war happened, and the whole thrust of *moledet* found a new focus of interest in the occupied territories. Interest in *yedi'at haaretz* acquired a tremendous boost, given added momentum by the growing religio-messianic attachment to Eretz Israel. The institutional framework of *moledet* was mobilized not only to conserve the newly acquired unspoiled landscape but actually as a means to take possession of it. It is no coincidence that one of the central features of many West Bank and Golan settlements are the field schools of the SPNI. As instructional centers for *moledet* they were in operation well before the settlements themselves and in some cases served as a guise for projected settlements. Extensive government-subsidized infrastructure and generous maintenance budgets have been in some cases a major income-generating branch of settlements that otherwise have no economic base.

Nature-reserve staff participate actively in government land acquisition. A special "Green Patrol," a paramilitary unit equipped with jeeps, radio communications, and weapons, patrols "state land," chases away Bedouins grazing their herds, and prevents "trespass" by Palestinian inhabitants. That operation is ostensibly aimed at preserving the vast "nature reserves" proclaimed by the military government. The authorities have harnessed *yedi'at haaretz* and the agencies charged with conservation to the operation of land seizure in the occupied territories. The "program for land seizure prepared by a decision of the Ministerial Committee for Settlement" in the West Bank specifies "afforestation, grazing area, and parks" as means to this end.

In the words of an official document, land seizure by creating parks and nature reserves is aimed at "the prevention of unsuitable development"—apparently by Arabs—but it is meant at the same time to "keep open the option of developing tourist enterprises at a later stage," thus "creating employment for the [Jewish] settlers." The phrasing of the purpose of parks is illuminating: "In *addition* to the benefits of seizing land, *other* benefits can be accrued, such as monetary profits, improvement of the quality of life *and* the environment, etc. [italics are author's]."

Jewish National Fund planners point out that "afforestation is a method of land seizure that can be implemented in areas that otherwise are difficult to seize." Thus school children taken by their teachers to plant trees in the occupied territories on Tu-Bishvat are fulfilling the full meaning of *yedi'at haaretz:* knowledge and possession. And in that, they are following a well-trodden path. Now, however, they are joined by new comrades: religious youth. After 1967 the secular cult of *moledet* acquired religio-messianic overtones. The students who attended yeshivas (religious academies), immersed in talmudic studies, excluded from the physical transformation of the country and the saga of statehood and development partly by choice and partly because of the monopoly of the secular sector, discovered *moledet* after 1967 and turned it into a fundamentalist myth.

Yedi'at haaretz had been an expression of revolt against the symbolism of *geographia sacra*—the sublimation of the earthly into the heavenly Jerusalem. It was a romantic, secular attempt to reach out to the primordial soil, to transform it and internalize it through study, art, and music, to create new, "normal" symbols. The religious Zionists clung to the spiritual meaning of the Holy Land. They could not and would not reject the utopic, messianic eschatological heritage of two thousand years of exile. This sublimated spiritual heritage became frozen in Jewish theology. Hence the basic concept of Zionism as embodied in *moledet*—a radical and revolutionary transformation of the situation of the Jewish people by transporting it to its own soil—seemed to the majority of religious Jews in the Diaspora simply blasphemous, preempting the coming of the Messiah. The minority of religious Zionists who came to the Holy Land and were forced to reconcile the heavenly with the earthly Jerusalem were then able to perceive the physical environment as a symbol of the supernatural, and the transformation of the landscape as a sign for the beginning of Redemption. However, the question of the involvement of religious Zionists in *moledet* remained unresolved, and most of them stayed aloof. It was the "miraculous" victory of the Six-Day War, the return to the Temple Mount, Bethel, and Hebron that produced in religious Jews a new messianic fervor. The younger generation of religious Zionists, restless for years and yearning for active participation in the ongoing national saga, perceived these events as the unfolding of a divine process in which they were not only permitted to take part but were actively called to be its spearhead.

With unrestrained zeal they set out to gain what they had lost in decades of exclusion. They found the secular establishment receptive and enthusiastic. After two generations of *moledet* the institutions created to support and sustain the love of the homeland were in deep crisis. The inherent weakness of *yedi'at haaretz* as a secular cult became apparent: it was a self-liquidating project. The immigrant founding fathers had created it with the intention of making their children indigenous—"an image of their homeland's landscape." In this they had been entirely successful, but in the process of instilling love for earthly Eretz Israel, the old symbolism, the spiritual heritage, was lost. In attaining reality they lost the dream, and the new symbols lacked depth; they were devoid of purpose except in themselves. This is normal. The annual American pilgrimage to New England to see the leaves in autumn is a value in itself. It is not perceived as a means to an ideological or spiritual end. But the Israeli educators were bound to perpetuate the cult of *moledet* because of a genuine feeling that the Zionist dream was still far from being realized: the majority of the Jewish people remain in the Diaspora; the land was not fully developed; and if young people are not sufficiently attached to their land, they may well emigrate. By this time as well the institutions of *moledet* had become vested interests, ends in themselves. There was also a nagging awareness that the obsession with cultivating rootedness after two generations meant one of two things: either a lack of confidence in the belongingness of Israelis in their land—or that the message had become banal through overrepetition and hence increasingly irrelevant to Israeli youth.

At this low point came the Six-Day War, reviving *moledet* and giving it a nationalistic-fundamentalist slant. The old secular symbols, long obsolete, were given a new lease on life, a new sense of purpose. The old establishment, and indeed a large segment of secular Israelis, have not understood the difference between a secular, nationalist-romantic cult and a cult based on the fulfillment of divine prophecies. The difference between the *madrichim* (guides) of *yedi'at haaretz*— nature enthusiasts, romantic explorers—and the religious zealots with a hot line to God who took over was simply overlooked.

It is significant that the politicization of *yedi'at haaretz* into an extremist, chauvinistic "Greater Israel" movement was carried out by the people most committed professionally or artistically to *moledet:* naturalists, guides, historians, topographers, novelists, and songwriters who had internalized the environment so thoroughly and depicted it so sensitively simply translated its emotional impact into political terms. They formed a strong bond with the religious fundamentalists under the banner of "the lovers of Eretz Israel," implying that all those who did not agree with their political platform were self-hating.

I return to my father, one of the architects of *moledet,* a kind, moderate person so far removed from right-wing excesses that the day Menachem Begin was elected prime minister was a day of mourning for him. One summer's day in 1983 he came back thrilled from traveling the length of the Jordan valley and seeing how the arid stretches of land had been transformed into fertile, productive soil. "Look what they are doing there," he enthused. "Making the desert bloom." It was a trip organized by the teachers' committee of the Jewish National Fund, and we were talking about forty thousand dunams of Arab property. Today, on the other side of the river, with the general improvement in security and the relaxation of tension, the Jordanians are also cultivating the soil—no less intensively and productively than we are—right to the river's edge. "Seventeen years ago," I answered my father, "the Arabs who had cultivated those fields were denied access for security reasons, and the land remained fallow. Now we've taken over. You call that making the desert bloom?" My father's response was immediate: "Of course it's making the desert bloom! What are you, for heaven's sake, a PLO sympathizer?"

I, his son, was involved in *moledet* from my fifth year onward, both as a student of *yedi'at haaretz* and as an active participant in the transformation of the environment. I shall return to the latter further on. When I turned eighteen I became a high priest in the cult of *moledet* complete with the romantic attire that went with it: a black embroidered *rubashka* (Russian blouse), a kaffiyeh (Arab headdress), army boots, and a map case. I knew the land, its contours, its wildlife, where to find water holes in the desert, and all the fortresses built by Flavius Josephus during the Great Revolt against the Romans. This land is part of me and I am part of it. Quite simply, my feeling for it is so great that I cannot stay abroad for more than a couple of months at a time. My American friends laugh when I tell them that the flowering trees in Central Park seem fake to me. Real trees can grow only in my land. My real scholarly discipline is the historical geography of the Holy Land.

Yet the area of specialization I chose for my academic studies reflected my revolt against the cult of *moledet.* I chose the Crusader period in Palestine, an unrelated episode in the history of the Holy Land but an integral and formative part in the history of Europe. Its connection to Jewish history is marginal, but its mark on the landscape of Israel is prominent. The magnificent castles, the impressive churches, the romantic place-names, the heroic chronicles captivated me. I was immersed in the feudal system, Church history, medieval symbolism, medieval architecture and art. I could study all that in direct relation to my own country.

I remember the day I told my father about my decision. A friend and professional colleague of his was present, and first to react. "Why the Crusaders?" he asked. "They massacred Jews in Europe and burned the entire Jewish community of Jerusalem. Can't you choose something connected with our presence here, like the Second Temple period?" For him, and for many, *moledet* is not just an academic vocation but rather an attempt to establish a claim. For me, apparently, the claim was obvious: it was based on the simple feeling of belonging in the land, of being there. I was not threatened by studying Catholic dogma lest I convert, nor was I haunted by anti-Semitic pogroms. I sought to explore the history and the monuments of my country irrespective of its ethnic connection. My vantage point was indigenous.

The study of the Crusaders became, years later, fashionable, because Arab scholars began to draw parallels between Zionism and the Crusades. I was also mobilized to write a pamphlet in which I vehemently denied the validity of the comparison. All such historical parallels are political battle cries, not serious analyses, but this particular one is absurd.

In my studies of the Crusader period I came across these words: *"Signor, faites au miex que vous poés que li tiere est perdu. Car je vuiderai le tiere, pour cou que je ne veul avoir reproce ne blasme, à le perdicion de le tiere."* ("Sire, do the best you can, for the land is lost. As for myself, I leave the land, because I do not want to be reproached and blamed for the loss of the land.") The speaker, Balian, Lord of Ibelin, one of the peers of the realm, a native Palestinian, uttered these arrogant and cowardly words in April 1187, and departed for Europe. Within three months the Latin Kingdom was utterly destroyed, Jerusalem and the Ibelin fief lost. From his refuge in France the renegade probably felt that his knightly honor was not compromised. After all, what can one man do in the face of such a calamity?

How foolish are the attempts to compare us to the Crusaders; how utterly absurd is the perception of us as a bunch of rootless drifters. The seedling, planted almost one hundred years ago, has grown into a robust and ramified tree, with roots deeply thrust in the soil of *moledet*. Unlike Balian, we have nowhere to go and no storm will uproot us. Yet we may dry up or rot from within. I copied Balian's words and hung them on my office wall as a warning.

In my time as a youth leader I must have taken thousands of teen-agers on hikes to the Galilee, to the wilderness of Judah, to the Negev canyons. Even now, middle-aged people whom I have not seen for thirty-five years enthuse when they recall this or that *tiyul* (hike) that I guided. I used to keep count of the times I climbed Massada together with youth groups. I stopped counting after the forty-third time. When in 1959 I collaborated with my father in writing a hiking guide for the Negev, my first published work, I dictated from memory complete hiking instructions for a five-day walking trip from Beersheba to Massada and a seven-day walking trip to Eilat: ". . . two roads lead from the north bank of Wadi Mor to Massada . . . the second is described here: in the dry wadi bed, one leaves the Sodom–Ein Gedi road and follows a path climbing on the north bank of the wadi, direction NW. Then the path turns N and climbs 400 meters in steep ascent. On the stony plateau the path leads NW. On both sides, ancient retaining walls built to facilitate the climb can be seen. After crossing the plateau (20 minutes) the path descends steeply to Wadi Rahaf. In the rocky bed, large water holes contain floodwater many weeks after the desert floods. One should replenish one's water supply here. . . . West of the Roman Camp Number 8, a path descends (steep slope, extreme caution) to the canyon of Wadi Seba (Massada), continuing along the wadi bed (some water holes) and encircling the rock of Massada, reaching the Roman siege ramp after 25 minutes.

Climbing a steep ascent on the ramp, one reaches the Plateau of Massada."

The *tiyul* was not just an outing. It was the high ceremony of the cult of *moledet*. The preparations took weeks and involved not only logistics such as transportation and food but rehearsals of performing troupes and preparations for evening lectures. Sometimes the logistics were quite esoteric. Before one *tiyul* in the early fifties we found we would not be able to maintain radio contact, so we got hold of a half-dozen pigeons, carried them on our backs, and released one each evening at sunset with a message attached to its leg. The *tiyul* itself was a test of endurance. We walked for days in temperatures that reached 42 degrees Celsius (108 degrees Fahrenheit). Water rationing was a particularly controversial feature of our *tiyulim*. In actual fact, children got sunstroke and there were even deaths from dehydration. One day, on the shores of the Dead Sea, a group leader reported to me that a water container had been stolen from his group that night. I demanded that the culprit identify himself, and when nobody spoke up, I told the entire group, eight hundred strong, to empty out their water supplies, leaving only one canteen per thirty people for emergencies. That day we walked twelve hours to Ein Gedi without drinking a single drop of water.

Later on it became clear that water rationing was positively dangerous. But all these hardships had ideological underpinnings. It was a cult, though a completely secular one. We had no need for religion, scoring it as a relic of Diaspora mentality. We would observe Yom Kippur by loading quantities of food onto a raft and swimming out with it to an offshore islet in the Mediterranean, and there we would while away the whole day feasting. It was a flagrant demonstration of our rejection of religious and Diaspora values. We saw ourselves forging a new culture, the culture of *moledet*.

The new culture can be described best by the myth of Massada. It is a particularly good example because it is an ancient Jewish symbol evoking memories of national struggle and heroism but is devoid of religious connotations. Massada is a typical product of the third aliyah, a wave of eastern European Jewish youth influenced by the socialist revolutionary ideas of the Russian Revolution of 1917. They created and elaborated the ethos of Massada, immortalized in a famous poem of that name by Yitzhak Lamdan. The line "Massada shall not fall again" became the battle cry of *moledet*. The siege of Massada, and not the destruction of the Temple, became our rallying point. It was to become a potent symbol, otherwise described as a complex, whose principal ingredients were that we are besieged and encircled, that the whole world is against us, and that we shall fight to the bitter end for national freedom and social justice.

However, the myth of Massada is unknown in Jewish sources. The episode became known only because Yosef Ben-Matitiyahu, alias Flavius Josephus, deserted his people while serving as the governor of Jewish Galilee and by an act of cowardice and duplicity went over to the Romans. Then he set out to write *The Jewish War*, which is no more and no less than an apologia justifying the tragedy of his people. His tales of Jewish heroism, Massada included, were narrated less from admiration for the Jewish fighters than from the desire to glorify the prowess of the Romans who defeated them. The work was preserved for us only because the Catholic Church saw in it the fulfillment of Jesus' warnings about the destruction of Jerusalem, the end of Old Israel, and the rise of the New Israel—the Christian faith. Jewish sources are totally silent about Massada, apparently because the mass suicide committed by its defenders is entirely alien to the spiritual characteristics that sustained the Jewish people in their land and after the destruction of the Temple, in the Diaspora. In any case, Massada as a symbol never gave the Jews in their plight any spiritual sustenance to survival because it was quite simply unknown.

Precisely because of that, it was a perfect myth for *moledet*. It canceled out two thousand years of Diaspora history and gave Israeli youth heroes and martyrs who died sword in hand for national freedom—just like a "normal" nation. The apocryphal speech of Elazar Ben-Yair, the commander of Massada, rang in our ears: "We were the first of all to revolt and shall be the last to break off the struggle—as we resolved at the beginning—we chose death rather than slavery.... Let us deny the enemy their hoped-for pleasure at our expense and without more ado leave them to be dumbfounded by our death and awed by our courage."

Approaching and climbing Massada in those days thirty years ago was usually a four- to five-day affair, as there was no passage for vehicles. I was deeply involved in elaborating this ethos. In 1953 I supervised the uncovering and reconstruction of the legendary "snake path," a tortuous, perilously steep path, unused since the siege, leading up Massada from the east. When we finished the work we ignited enormous "fire inscriptions" made from kerosene-soaked rags. The entire path was lit up by torches, and colorful tracer bullets were shot from the mountaintop. Yet around the campfire later that night I could not help expressing my doubts about the whole exercise. It was, I think, a memorable night not only for me but for all those who participated in that discussion.

My friend and mentor Yehuda Almog, perhaps the archetype of the third aliyah, who came to the Dead Sea in the late twenties and stayed, spoke to our group on the meaning of Massada. Unable to remain silent, I remember getting up and saying that although I had been raised on the myth of Elazar Ben-Yair, in my judgment—speaking as a Jew and as an Israeli—it was Rabban Yochanan Ben-Zakkai who was truly a national hero and not the half-demented refugees who committed suicide. Here was a man, a great and compassionate teacher, who realized at the height of the Roman siege of Jerusalem that if the slaughter continued, nothing whatsoever would be left of the Jewish people. He was smuggled into the Roman camp from the besieged city in a coffin, approached Titus, and negotiated an agreement with him. As a result of this, he and other scholars were permitted to settle in the town of Yavneh. There they created a spiritual and intellectual center that really saved the remnant of the Jewish people after the destruction of the Temple.

It is natural that Elazar Ben-Yair is a hero to the Israeli people. But for two thousand years of exile from their homeland, the person who created the religious, spiritual, and social conditions for sustaining the Jewish people in Israel and in the Diaspora, without the Temple, was Ben-Zakkai. True, the rosters of priestly duty were maintained, scholarly learning pertaining to the priesthood and sacrifices continued. Every detail was scrupulously preserved. Tractates would be written on the regalia of the high priest, the sacrifices, the tithe. But the scholars of Yavneh brought about a situation in which only the Messiah could purify the Holy Site, thus perhaps inadvertently removing to a misty and indefinite future the possibility of reestablishing the Temple cult.

Throughout history, Yavneh was and continued to be a symbol for religious Jewry. But this stream of Jewry had no significance for modern Israel. Massada, seen as an act of desperate courage, was, on the other hand, a most compelling symbol. The mass suicide was interpreted not as an act of self-destruction but as an act of defiance—a heroic last stand in defense of their vow to live as free men in their homeland. But, I argued, to model the Jewish people after the Italian or the Czech struggle for national liberation, which the Massada symbol implied, must backfire on us simply because one cannot erase two thousand years of history and ignore the connection between our religious heritage and the new secular nationalism. Italians and Czechs may evoke the memory of past grandeur, but it does not entail the same inseparable bond between religious and national symbols, and the tribal tradition, three millennia old, that obliges everyone to regard himself as though he personally had gone forth from Egypt.

Even Massada was not garrisoned and defended for abstract national reasons alone, but for both religious and national reasons at the same time. Ben-Yair declared, "We resolved . . . [not] to serve . . . anyone else but only God, who alone is the true and righteous Lord of Men."

As we have seen since, the religious context was too powerful to be ignored, and it ultimately transformed the secular ethos into a chauvinistic-fundamentalist cult. Yochanan Ben-Zakkai's teachings—that the supreme symbol of Judaism, the Holy Temple in Jerusalem, can never be rebuilt by human agency but must remain a national and religious ideal to which we shall always aspire but never attain except by Divine Providence whose ways are unknown to us—have been impatiently swept aside. By restoring Massada as a secular alternative to the Temple (which in any case was not then in our hands) we, as it turned out later, unleashed forces that would demand the restoration of the true symbol of religious and national unity—Mount Moriah—the Temple itself.

But this was to happen later. In the late fifties and early sixties Massada became a national shrine. Archaeological excavations revealed the accuracy of Josephus's narrative and gave the myth added credibility. The Israeli Army provided the logistics, and thousands of volunteers from all over the world flocked to participate in excavating and restoring the site. Massada was declared a national monument. The dramatic torch-lit ceremony on Massada in which thousands of army conscripts swore allegiance to the state and the armed forces completed the picture.

With all my misgivings, which at the time I attributed to my own internal contradictions and are now reinforced by the wisdom of hindsight, I participated actively in all of that. As chairman of a governmental agency charged with the development of the Dead Sea region, I supervised the construction of a youth hostel at the foot of Massada, as well as an airstrip, roads, and water supply. We made that harsh, inhospitable area an easily accessible tourist attraction. At the time I did not know that all this was but a prelude to what came to pass a few years later in 1967.

In June 1967, following the Six-Day War, the secular ethos of Massada came in direct contact with the supreme symbol of Judaism—the Temple Mount. The fusion triggered a chain reaction that threatens to take on cataclysmic proportions. I came to the Western Wall almost with the first paratrooper units in midmorning of June 7, 1967. A good deal has been said about the return to the Wall and the Temple Mount. In a book I wrote not long after the event I said, "[It was] an experience so powerful that it had few parallels, even in the chronicles of such an ancient people. It deeply affected the Jewish people as a whole and every one of its members singly. For the devout, it was the beginning of redemption; cynics and atheists suddenly found themselves linked again into a long chain of generations that had whispered, 'Next year in Jerusalem.' It was a religious experience in the true sense of the term."

The tragic history of the Jewish people can be read in two seemingly paradoxical signs displayed at the gates to the Holy Enclosure: one, a stone inscription in Greek from the first century A.D.; the other, a metal plaque from 1967. The ancient Herodian inscription warns all *gentiles* on penalty of death to stay away from the sacred precincts. The modern inscription, signed by the Israeli Chief Rabbinate, warns *Jews* that under Halakah (religious law) it is forbidden to set foot on the Temple Mount.

Two thousand years ago the Jewish people not only lost their Temple, the supreme symbol of their faith, but eventually also deprived themselves of the right to enter its precincts, let alone rebuild it. The Temple Mount remained "full of the honor of the Lord God of Israel and His sanctity." So sacred is this area that according to Jewish law no one will be ritually fit to enter it until the coming of the Messiah and the restoration of the rite of purification.

The emotional burden shouldered by every Jew conscious of his history, whether religious or not, when standing at the gates of the Temple Mount is almost beyond description. The vanished glory of the Temple recalled with passionate

yearning in talmudic literature, the solemnity and sanctity
of the rituals performed by the priests in the Sanctuary, and
above all the terrible moment of the Temple's destruction
are etched deeply in the Jewish psyche: "Then one of the
Roman soldiers . . . snatched up a blazing piece of wood and
climbing on another soldier's back hurled the brand through
a golden aperture . . . the Temple Hill, enveloped in flames
from top to bottom, appeared to be boiling up from its very
roots."

Israeli school pupils commit to memory the searing images
in Bialik's epic, *The Scroll of Fire*, of the "Lord God of Ven-
geance, He Himself, calm and terrible, sitting on a throne of
fire in the heart of the blazing sea," and the Angel of Hope:
"And one young angel, sad-eyed and white-winged, the
Guardian of the Pearls of the Hidden Tear in the Cup of Mute
Sorrow, saw above Aurora, a fire-curl, the remnant of Ariel,
the perpetual fire, flickering, trembling and dying amongst
the scorched altar stones on the Temple Mount. . . . And he
hastened and flew above Aurora . . . and snatched the Lord's
fire . . . held it close to his heart, touching it with his lips
. . . and brought it to a desolate island and placed it on a
promontory. Aloft he lifted his sad eyes, and his lips whispered in silence: God of Mercy and Deliverance, let your last
ember not be extinguished forever."

Mercy and deliverance. That was the feeling shared by
the scores of soldiers gathered in the narrow, shaded alley
in front of the Wall, the remnant of our Temple. It is no
accident that the photograph immortalizing the Six-Day War
is of a young paratrooper holding a helmet in his hands and
lifting up his sad eyes. We watched in silence the chief army
chaplain placing a bench in front of the Wall, holding up a
Torah scroll, and then blowing the shofar. The symbolic significance of these acts was well known to older soldiers who
had been forbidden to do any of these things by the British
authorities because they were "offensive to the Muslims." It
was a sign that the dream of worshipping without harassment at our most sacred place had been realized after

223 months of Jordanian occupation and 1897 years of exile. I remembered the last time I visited the Wall; it was on Yom Kippur, 1947, twenty years before. We, members of a secular youth movement, were not interested in the services. We came to participate in a patriotic demonstration: to defy the British. The narrow alley was packed with worshippers and encircled by British troops, both sides waiting for the cue: the blowing of the ram's horn signaling the end of the Day of Atonement. A young Jew takes out the shofar and puts it to his mouth. He succeeds in blowing the first wailing sounds, a squad of British soldiers jumps from an adjacent building on the worshippers and grabs the boy, the crowd sings *"Hatikvah,"* some are taken away, we march back through the dark alleys and sing nationalistic songs.

That morning in 1967 I touched the cold stones and left. Only many hours later, when I listened to the official announcement on the radio, did I realize what had happened. When I heard Moshe Dayan's words—"We have returned to our most holy places; we have returned and we shall never leave them"—I burst into tears. It was only later, much later, that we all realized what forces had been unleashed by the return to our most holy places. We were still thinking and acting in the context of secular *moledet,* and were confident that we could ride the storm.

When I returned to the *Kotel* (the Western Wall) three days later, the whole area in front of the Wall was a heap of ruins. Bulldozers had toppled the one- and two-story houses of the Mugrabi Quarter, inhabited by some one hundred Arab families. They were ordered to evacuate their dwellings so that ample space could be provided at the Wall for the anticipated tens of thousands of Jewish pilgrims. In charge of the operation I found my old colleagues from Massada—Mayor Teddy Kollek, an archaeologist, an architect, and a specialist on the preservation of historic sites. Teddy Kollek, who as director-general of the prime minister's office was responsible for the restoration of Massada, summoned his former aides, and as mayor of Jerusalem was deep in creating a new historic monument—the Western Wall plaza.

As I read my own account written in the early seventies, it is surprising now that at the time I thought the following questions "pertinent": "Who decided that the Western Wall has a purely religious character? Was it not a national historic relic? Was the Wall solely a place to express religious feelings?" It is even more surprising that the secular establishment assumed that it would be able to maintain control over the Wall under the aegis of the National Parks Authority! The secular myth of Massada was apparently very strong, but the religio-messianic fervor was stronger. It has to be admitted that the attempt to carry the secular nationalistic concept of *moledet* over to the Temple Mount was a *reductio ad absurdum*. The Chief Rabbinate not only won jurisdiction over the *Kotel* but transformed it into an Orthodox synagogue, separating men and women. The secular claim over the Western Wall died quietly. The secular establishment diverted its efforts to an area south and southeast of the praying area, excavated and restored it. The religious establishment, not content with the traditional praying area, began an elaborate dig under existing Muslim buildings with the intention of "uncovering the whole length of the Western Wall." All the underground vaults cleared of the debris of centuries were immediately converted into Orthodox synagogues. One day a building whose foundations were undermined by the dig threatened to crumble. Municipal employees under my direction tried to shore up the building and leaned the supporting beams on the Wall. Within a very short time a large group of ultrareligious Jews gathered, chased the workers away, and began to collect small stones that they claimed had been detached from the sacred wall. Afterward, they carried away the stones, collected in large jars, "for burial." Watching that pagan procession, spellbound, I recalled, by contrast, the way the Ashkenazic chief rabbi, Avraham Yitzhak Hacohen Kook, had explained the significance of the Western Wall to the first British governor of Jerusalem in 1920: "The Western Wall especially has survived as a sign and as a token of our redemption and of the certainty of our return to the sacred standing. . . . We have no interest in the stones or from which period they date. For us, the main thing is the place and the holy air above it, up to the height of heaven . . ."

The underground dig had been carried out without permission from the competent authorities in charge of planning and antiquities and without the consent of the Muslim property owners. My efforts to regulate this illegal operation, carried out by a government ministry, won me the name "Arab lover." As recently as 1984, a journalist from a religious newspaper told his readers how I "gave advice to the head of the Muslim Waqf [religious endowment] on how to claim ownership over the historic vaults near the Western Wall" and this was proof of my continued role as "patron of the Arabs."

But all this had been marginal, almost comical, compared with the real drama that took place above the Wall on the Temple Mount itself.

On the morning of Saturday, June 17, 1967, I watched the supreme product of *moledet*, Moshe Dayan, confronted with the Holy of Holies. This man, Moshe Dayan, found himself not only confronted with the enormous emotional burden but was also, in particular terms, forced to decide how to deal with the question of "possession" of this holy site that had been taken over by the believers of another religion thirteen hundred years ago. This was *moledet*'s finest hour. I watched Dayan taking off his shoes before entering al-Aqsa Mosque. This gesture did not escape the tense Muslim clergymen: the Jew had acknowledged their possession. He retained his prerogatives as a governor but did not rob them, as a Jew, of what the Muslims considered their own after having held the area for over a millennium.

This historic decision has been upheld by all Israeli governments ever since. Through this consistency, a bearable coexistence between Jews and Muslims could be maintained in the holy city. But the pressures on that rational, sensible policy have been enormous. It can be maintained only as long as the Chief Rabbinate adheres to the unambiguous ruling that Jews are forbidden entry—lest they inadvertently violate the place where the original Holy of Holies stood, a place that can no longer be pinpointed.

This ruling is challenged by those who claim that they can identify the different sections of the Temple area. They maintain that the southern section of the Holy Enclosure is outside the ancient Temple area, and therefore an Orthodox Jew can enter it after performing purification rites. On the pilgrimage festivals of Passover, Shavuoth, and Sukkoth, and on the ninth day of the month of Av (the day both the First and the Second Temple were destroyed), groups of extremist Jews, nationalist rather than religious, try to conduct prayer services on the southern area of the Temple Mount. Israeli police prevent them from entering or expel the worshippers who succeed in infiltrating. These attempts, intended to demonstrate "Jewish rights of ownership," are a constant nuisance. But they seem naïve compared to the fundamentalist-messianic drive to actually destroy the mosques and prepare for the resumption of the ancient cult on the Temple Mount.

Since 1967 a number of attempts to harm the mosques on the Temple Mount have been perpetrated. The most serious attempt was uncovered in 1984 by Israeli security forces, and the perpetrators, members of a fundamentalist-chauvinistic Jewish underground, were put on trial. One of them stated from the witness stand, "I state that I see myself compelled to prepare an action, which I term purification of the Temple Mount—the only holy place of the people in Israel—by the removal of the building situated on its summit, on the site of the Holy of Holies, the building known as the Dome of the Rock. . . . The Temple Mount must not only be in our hands as a focal point of our sovereignty; indeed, gentiles are forbidden to tread on it, and needless to say, to control it. It must be turned into the central place, radiating holiness and strength to the entire country and to all the Jewish people." After one of the criminals received a ten-year sentence for his part in the plot, his father shouted: "From the list of so-called accusations, the most important one has been omitted: *Ahavat Eretz Israel* [Love for Eretz Israel]."

Moledet is brought to its final destination. The genie we flirted with during our desert hikes came out of the bottle. Massada, the direct link we forged with our distant, heroic past, had been replaced by Mount Moriah. Our attempt to eradicate the painful memories of our exile and Diaspora had given license to destroy what others did in this land in our absence, to chase the gentiles away and restore the temple cult. Our boundless preoccupation with the physical landscape and our perception of the Arabs as objects in that landscape unwittingly contributed to the loss of humanitarian values. With our adulation of development, our habit of attaching transcendental values to human creations in concrete and steel, to every grove of trees planted, we paved the way to a new form of Jewish paganism, and for an exotic growth of believers in the End of the Days. Our obsession with instilling *moledet*, together with our negligence of equally cherished values such as the brotherhood of man, social justice and civil equality to all, had lead inexorably to chauvinism and xenophobia.

It is tempting to take the easy way out and dismiss the right-wing chauvinists and religious fundamentalists as an aberration, as marginal, half-crazed fanatics. Yet very influential sections of Israeli public opinion accept their philosophy, albeit considering them "good boys who slipped." It is easy to absolve ourselves by laying the blame on others who by their demagoguery pushed the country in a new and sinister direction that "we" were powerless to prevent despite "our" best efforts. As an active participant in the cult of *moledet*, as a son of one of its creators, I must reflect on our share in the shame. As I listen to the expressions and watch the symbols, I discern the twisted, deformed symbols of my youth. I see the fallen pillars of my temple, scorched by a strange fire.

Was it predetermined in the very concept of *moledet?* I don't think so. We were aware of its inherent contradictions and conflicting values. For a time we were able to reconcile them, but we did not have the courage to cry "halt" in time. We did not have the wisdom to see how the reality we created transformed the meaning of our petrified ethos without affecting its external shell. We were loyal to the bitter end. The causes for this loyalty, and how it was ingrained in us, require further elaboration.

3

Denouement

One afternoon last winter we drove down yet again to Zorah to bury a friend. Only a year ago we buried Mussa. Now Yankaleh's grave waited next to his in the small cemetery of the kibbutz we all helped establish one winter day in 1949. The first kibbutz of our generation.

Middle-aged men and women assembled quietly on the lawn near the dining hall, inspecting one another minutely, noticing the physical changes wrought by the passing years, trying to hide their melancholy by slapping each other on the shoulder, Israeli style; few wore *kipot* (yarmulkes) as required at funerals. Our antireligious sentiment was still strong. People came from everywhere, from all parts of the country, from all walks of life, some in chauffeur-driven limousines, many in kibbutz working clothes; almost all of us Israeli-born from urban, middle-class, Ashkenazic homes, we were members of the same youth movement, burying a comrade in the shrine of our youth, the kibbutz. We were a caste, the sons and daughters of a revolutionary elite, beautiful, strong, in love with ourselves. A narcissist society. We sacrificed our lives to realize the Zionist ideals and ingrain socialist values in masses of new immigrants. Therefore, nothing was too good for us. We were the *crème de la crème*.

We walked slowly in a long procession between the attractive homes and gardens up the hill of Zorah, Samson's birthplace, mentioned in the Book of Judges: "And the spirit of the Lord began to move him at times in the camp of Dan, between Zorah and Eshtaol."

As we assembled around the grave, freshly dug among the pines that we planted thirty-five years ago, the atmosphere became oppressive. Many wept openly. Ketzaleh began speaking in a low voice. As he eulogized Yankaleh, our dead friend from my kibbutz, Rosh Haniqra, I suddenly recalled the eulogy I gave at Tumi's funeral. Tumi, another comrade of Ketzaleh's, from Kibbutz Nahal Oz. Tumi, my roommate in the commune in Rehovot, killed by the Egyptians in the fifties. I stood next to my brother Rafi, my friends Ronnie, Adina, Kochka, and Uzi, who welcomed me the day I came to join the kibbutz in November 1952. As I listened to Ketzaleh's eulogy in the company of my comrades, I suddenly realized that it was a whole era and shared experience that we were really laying to rest. Upon the marble tombstone should be engraved the epitaph of our youthful ideals, the demise of an elite.

Ketzaleh, now a member of the Knesset, spoke about Yankaleh, the kibbutznik who died as chairman of the board of one of the hundred largest banks in the world. "A giant among dwarfs," said Ketzaleh. "We always knew that even when you wore a suit and tie [traditionally anathema to us in the kibbutz movement], and took upon yourself those mighty, superhuman tasks [his reference was to international finance], you were, underneath it all, still dressed in the blue shirt with its red lacing [our youth movement uniform], and on your back the knapsack, ready to ascend the mountain. . . .

"This was not a man but a rocket," continued Ketzaleh. "His fuel was comradeship, and when it ran short, nothing was left." We knew right away what Ketzaleh meant: the solidarity and belongingness that nourished all of us from the kibbutz movement as though we were a tribe.

"Just thirty years ago, in the youth movement, we would sing, 'We shall array thy form in a robe of concrete and cement.' This was the pioneer ideal. Yankaleh took this with the utmost seriousness: to do, to build, create and forge new contents for the concepts of state, movement, and society. ... We stand dazzled before the burgeoning of the workers' cooperatives, the industrial enterprises, agriculture, tourism, universities—all issuing forth as if by magic touch—all this creativity is his living memorial—the real gravestone under which Yankaleh lies with his spirit hovering above—and no one can take these achievements from you. You were a marvel of a man who, eaglelike, soared high beyond us carrying on your outstretched wings the economy of the entire movement—a kind of Titan ... people may pass on, but their deeds remain."

The rhetoric was high-flown even by the standard of eulogies. But this too was typical of us. We tend to be plain, even coarse, in our everyday speech but flowery and bombastic in our public addresses. It seemed appropriate and even moving. The burial prayers were uttered almost in whispers. Yankaleh's sons read the Kaddish. Before departing, we shook hands, knowing that most of us would meet again only when another comrade is laid to rest. I drove home, sat alone in the dark, and for hours just played the old tunes: the Israeli ballads and dances of our youth, sentimental Russian folk songs, Hassidic Sabbath melodies. Everything I used to play with Yankaleh, he on the accordion and I on my twin harmonicas, one in C, one in A flat. And I wept over my dreams, the shattered vessels of our youth.

During the past few years, we—my generation—began reaching the age of fifty. It began to dawn on us that we had fulfilled our functions—the biological ones, certainly—and were approaching the end of the road. And looking back we became aware that our generation, the generation of sons for whom our parents had spared no effort, on whom they had focused all their aspirations, this generation had turned out to be a lost generation, wanderers in the wilderness. We compared ourselves with the generation of founders and were diminished by the comparison. Our contribution has in sum turned out to be relatively marginal—with notable exceptions, of course, such as the army, technology, perhaps in the arts. But the best hopes of our parents were invested in our generation. We aspired to the creation of a new and better society. We wanted a country based on pioneering values and social justice. My generation, to a great extent, simply abandoned the struggle.

We have renounced the struggle for a new type of humanity. We have been able to produce a modern, self-sustaining, technological society but have not managed to establish new social values and to cultivate new human relationships. This is in effect the journey we have made—from the early pioneer ethos to a consumer society, dominating another nation. How it came about is our subject here.

One becomes painfully aware that one is really witnessing a movement eulogizing itself, marking its own demise. Because when you came down to it, these people—all of us—are fully aware in our heart of hearts that the genuine aim of our education was to create a better form of social framework within which human beings could function on a higher plane. I traveled the same path, along with all these people.

Our emotions at the funeral were in part a recognition that the ideology that had sustained us and in which we, the second generation of Israelis, were educated can serve us no longer in facing the problems that confront us. It is quite simply fossilized, frozen. It froze at a point at which many ideologically motivated movements freeze, when they could not adapt to changing realities.

Naturally we tried to perceive it in the context of the old, vital ideology. So Yankaleh, the international financier and banker, sitting in boardrooms in his dark suit and tie, remained, as Ketzaleh said, "dressed in the blue shirt with its red lacings." But the truth is that Ketzaleh's funeral oration, with its emphasis on concrete, material achievements, could just as well have been delivered over a Rockefeller's grave. It is the combination of the bankers' ethos with the blue shirt that renders it pathetic.

Late at night I have a habit of turning to Radio Belgrade because they play the "Internationale" at the end of their broadcasts. Sentimental? Vain yearnings for the aspirations of my youth? Perhaps. But then many of my generation have been abandoned the sentiment. The last time I attended a Labor Party Congress they played the "Internationale," as is traditional. And I looked around and found that only I and a couple of friends of mine were singing. The orchestra played and the choir sang—and an audience of two thousand, without a clue as to what the words were, just stood there shuffling their feet in embarrassment. The "Internationale" was a hymn, an anthem to the dawn of a new life, a statement of faith in the possibility of creating a better world, a just society —whether through Marxism, social democracy, or liberalism was immaterial.

And hence we believed in the words with the utmost sincerity. We sang it, together with *"Hatikvah,"* our national anthem, and our ten-year-olds in the youth movement stood at attention. Curiously, I even remember the day in 1941 when the Soviet Union abandoned the "Internationale" as its national anthem and replaced it with a new patriotic song. I was six years old! Not only that, I still possess the battered pamphlet of the *Communist Manifesto* from which I read the immortal line. "The worker has nothing to lose except his chains" to my youth group, aged twelve, myself already the ripe old age of fifteen.

All this can be dismissed as a belated expression of disillusionment with socialism, so fashionable in Europe in the forties and fifties. We, of course, shared this sentiment caused by the agonies and defeats of the socialist movement: the Spanish Civil War, Nazism, Fascism, Communist totalitarianism. Yet we were different from other socialist movements elsewhere. Their aim had been to transform society; our task was to create one.

Our ideology rested on the twin pillars of Zionism and socialism. Indeed the amalgamation of the cult of labor and the struggle for statehood, the blue-and-white flag and the red banner, the farmer and the fighter, *"Hatikvah"* and the "Internationale" is the essence of the pioneering ethos. There were, of course, other ideologies, but ours dominated the Zionist movement and Israel for two generations. It is ingrained in the pioneering image of Israel, and in the awe-inspiring personalities of David Ben-Gurion and Golda Meir. Those who embraced the Zionist ideals have indirectly been affected by its socialist message even if they loathe and deny it.

Massada and kibbutz, two symbols around which our lives evolved. The secular nationalistic symbol, and the nucleus of the new and just world. *Moledet* instilled love for the homeland. *Hagshama* educated us to participate in the realization of the socialist dream. *Hagshama* literally means "realization," both of self and on the collective level. Our perception of realization had perhaps no parallel in any other society except in monastic orders, Christian or Buddhist. It meant total personal commitment to a way of life—kibbutz life. We were not taught nor did we teach our youth how to conduct their lives in an open, heterogeneous society. Education in values of good citizenship or participating in the struggle against social inequality were secondary. Our aim was to develop groups of highly motivated activists who would settle in the kibbutz, the agrarian commune, the only effective instrument for the realization of Zionist ideals.

An educational system broadly based on love of country and good citizenship leaves you free to choose your livelihood and way of life with the proviso that whatever you do, you will do honestly and well. But *hagshama* effectively closed off all options but one: a lifelong commitment to kibbutz life, the highest ideal to which man could aspire. That lofty and total dedication gave our activities a truly cosmic significance.

Naturally, it required a solid ideological and emotional basis. After all, most of us were sons and daughters of middle-class, relatively settled town-dwellers. Our parents were past their pioneering phase. They had returned from the reclaimed swamps and citrus groves to join the swelling bureaucracies of the Zionist and trade union institutions. Concerning us, they were torn between conflicting desires. They wanted us to participate in *hagshama*, for they identified with the ethos, yet they wished that we complete our formal education and prepare for academic or professional careers. When I was sixteen I wanted to leave school and join a kibbutz. My mother convinced me to stay. "Kibbutzniks must be educated people," she said. "You'll be more useful there if you finish school." Much later I realized how they reconciled their conflicting desires: they exposed us to public indoctrination of Labor-Zionist ideology but still relied on their personal influence and middle-class values. Their contradictory educational objectives had, as we shall see, long-lasting effects on us.

Two public institutions participated in our socialization to the pioneering ethos: the school and the youth movement. The school curriculum instilled in us *moledet*, and the youth movement, *hagshama* values.

The socialist ideological frameworks that sustained *hagshama* were diverse. The bitter controversies that tore the Israeli labor movement caused ideological strife and fragmentation. Some groups were Marxist, the others non-Marxist. The ideology that illuminated our path was decidedly non-Marxist. Although we were profoundly influenced by Karl Marx, we sought to emphasize "humanistic socialism" as opposed to this "scientific," deterministic philosophy. Our ideology had been a curious mixture of Jewish values of social justice, the legacy of our Prophets, anarchist hatred for the coercive power of the state, contempt for middle-class values and for the modern, atomized society. In fact, it was aimed at justifying kibbutz life as the model of social justice and not merely as an instrument for the realization of Zionism.

We belonged to the stream in socialism termed by Marx and Engels "utopian" as opposed to their "scientific" philosophy. We believed in free choice and voluntary action as opposed to Marxist determinism. For us the communal village was the prototype of the new social order. Communities of people determined to realize in their daily life the principles of social justice would be the vanguard of socialism. They would radiate their influence on the atomized urban society and reconstruct it along socialist lines. Faced with the failure of previous attempts to establish socialist communities— from Thomas More's *Utopia* to more recent attempts in the Old and the New World—we sought to explain the difference between utopia and the Israeli kibbutz. Martin Buber, the great Jewish religious philosopher, provided the answer along with an attractive justification for leaving our parents' cozy home. In an essay that we learned almost by heart, titled "The Experiment That Has Not Failed," Buber described the reasons for the phenomenal success of the Israeli cooperative villages compared with the total failure of other utopian experiments.

As Buber saw it, the nonfailure (he was not prepared to see the kibbutz as an unqualified success) stemmed from the nondoctrinaire character of these settlements. The kibbutz, he argued, was conditioned by necessity. Unlike other utopian communities, it was not a product of a theory but rather "a product of a condition—social distress, dire necessity." In the first Israeli communes "ideological imperatives were combined with the need of the hour" to create a magnificent amalgamation. The ideological element "preserved almost completely its soft, flexible character." There were many futuristic dreams. Some viewed the kibbutz as a new and comprehensive form of a family; some regarded themselves as the vanguard of the labor movement and even as the actual realization of socialism, a prototype of the new society. Some saw in it the beginning of the creation of a new humanity and a brave new world. "Nothing, however, was frozen into a solid dogma: the ideal created necessity but not dogma; it encouraged, not dictated." But more important, argued Buber, behind the condition that determined the role of the kibbutz

stood an historic situation—the situation of a people that suffered a great external crisis and reacted with a great internal revolution; and this historic situation created an elite, the pioneering elite. The form of life most appropriate for this elite was the communal settlement. This form was most appropriate for executing the central functions of pioneering. It was also the form that enabled the socialist ideal to penetrate into the core of the national idea. . . . The elite and its way of life could not remain isolated or stagnant. Its functions, enterprises, pioneering spirit made it a center of gravity, loaded it with electric currents—transferring energy and influencing the entire society in a positive and constructive way.

By *hagshama*, self-realization, we joined the elite and therefore became potential political leaders, part of the "chosen few." Milking the cows in the kibbutz possessed not only cosmic significance, it brought us closer to the political power center—a very attractive combination for ambitious young persons who leave their parents' cozy homes.

It goes without saying that the objectives to which we educated our juniors in the youth movement were based on personal example. Only those who had chosen to live in a kibbutz could lead others. Therefore it was at a very immature stage of our lives that we had the tremendous burden of contending with our own difficulties in adjusting to our chosen way of life as well as the responsibility of actively preparing younger cohorts to emulate us. There was enormous temerity and arrogance in forging a commitment of this magnitude in the minds of young children, regardless of whether the life of an agrarian commune held the slightest interest for them. Perhaps only acolytes in a monastic order, and then not invariably, are able to subdue their own personal desires and individuality to the rules laid down for them. But when I was growing up, in the circles in which I moved, there was no hesitation. It was taken for granted that all of us would either move to a kibbutz or found one of our own. Anybody who didn't, simply didn't count.

We regarded young people who belonged to what we called "drawing room society," attached to bourgeois comforts and passing fashions, with the utmost contempt. We had an elitist conception of ourselves as cadres in the battle for a socialist society. We, the blue-shirted pioneers of laboring Israel, regarded ourselves as kings of all we surveyed.

We derided—often viciously—the other youth movements. The Scouts, for example. They were supposed to do a good deed a day. Their ideological horizons were just broad enough to escort old ladies across the street. We, on the other hand, had no time for a good deed a day because we were revolutionaries; we were creating the socialist cells that would eventually transform the whole of society.

This description of the pioneering youth movement should not mislead the reader into thinking of us as a group of young ideologues. Side by side with soul-searching debates, we were plunged into social and cultural activities that forged lasting personal relationships. We made the most daring hikes, our dance groups were the best, our girls the prettiest. In fact, membership in the youth movement forged social ties that resemble, surprisingly, the "old boy" network of graduates of British aristocratic boarding schools. One can rely all one's life on a comrade. Members of the same group find themselves living in the same neighborhood, belonging to the same army reserve unit, meeting socially.

Our uncompromising standards, our total commitment, our comradeship, the shared hardships and ideological struggles truly were extraordinary. Perhaps they were superhuman. Because, in the end, they defeated us. How many people can stand by a decision made at the age of sixteen and meant to determine the whole future course of their lives?

I am a typical example. In November 1952 I joined, together with my comrades, Kibbutz Rosh Haniqra on the Israeli-Lebanese border. The reality of kibbutz life was totally at odds with my expectations. I remember those backbreaking early dawns harvesting clover with a sickle. I earnestly tried to perceive the cosmic meaning of my work but could feel only deadly boredom, and at the same time shame and disappointment at my weakness. I longed for intellectual challenges, but my physical exhaustion left me unable to read a page in the evening. I dreaded the sound of the gong waking us for another day in the fields. I was simply not cut out for the life of the agrarian society.

For a while I worked as a youth leader in Tel Aviv and lived in a commune educating new groups. Then one day I got on a bus, arriving at my kibbutz in midmorning when most people were out in the fields, and simply notified the kibbutz office that I was leaving. I did not take anything with me, just a terrible feeling of shame. I have a vivid recollection of walking slowly down that unpaved road, hoping not to meet any of my comrades, of boarding a bus and going directly to the registrar's office of the Hebrew University in Jerusalem. For twenty-five years I never went back to Rosh Haniqra. I understood that I was a renegade, that I had committed the unforgivable sin of betraying *hagshama* when I decided that kibbutz life was no longer for me and perhaps never had been. When I realized that agrarian, communal life simply did not allow me sufficient latitude to express my own personality, I was placed in a double bind: betrayal of my own ideals and values, and betrayal of my comrades and the hundreds of teen-agers who took me seriously and acted upon my words. But worse, the personal feeling of inadequacy, the burning shame of not being strong enough to live up to my own standards and beliefs, left in me a deep emotional scar that has never really healed.

It is ironic that all these agonies were, even then, in 1953–54, anachronistic. Our total commitment to the kibbutz as the perfect instrument for the realization of both Zionism and socialism blinded us. We did not understand that the newly born State of Israel was faced with problems that required a new national agenda, and in that agenda the role of our perception of *hagshama* was marginal.

It was David Ben-Gurion who was the first to understand that the old ethos is obsolete. Confronted with the urgent needs of creating a state, absorbing mass immigration, and building an economy, he could not allow all ideologically motivated, college-educated youth to go to kibbutzim. He redefined *hagshama* and legitimized new forms of pioneering:

in the new state ministries, in the new professional army, and in other bureaucratic jobs. He hoisted a new flag, the flag of *mamlachtiut*, "statism." Ben-Gurion did not dare fold away the red socialist flag, but while he continued to pay lip service to socialist ideals, he changed the priorities. In the process, he did not flinch from slaughtering our sacred cows: the Palmach —the kibbutz-commanded elite army unit—was disbanded and integrated into the new state army; the socialist schools were disbanded and incorporated in the state school system. We regarded all this as a betrayal of our ideals and termed statism "careerism." Suddenly, it seemed, one could be a pioneer and realize Zionist ideals out of a cozy office in Tel Aviv. We resented the new definition of *hagshama*.

When my officers in the army selected me to attend officers' training school, I refused to go. When I received a direct order, I had no choice but to sit for entrance exams. I filled in the forms with "I don't want to be an officer." The army put me in custody for a week for "destroying military property," then released me to go back to my kibbutz. Afterward, the army gave us the right to nominate candidates for officers' training.

The shift of priorities was inevitable. But we were caught unprepared, and felt betrayed and confused. There were long-term results to our confusion.

Many of us abdicated completely the social role for which we had prepared ourselves. Professor Yishayahu Leibowitz foresaw the danger in a penetrating essay written in 1953.

Education in pioneering values aimed at creating a new society had largely given way to technical and vocational training, he wrote. There was an attempt to incorporate training for a career, whether in the professions or in the army, into the pioneering ethos by means of various slogans that underwent changes according to the exigencies of the moment. Once it was "The best . . . to the kibbutz." Then it was "The best to the air force," followed in quick succession by the army, electronics, and other careers. Of course we were not so naïve and utopian as to not comprehend the need for trained personnel and an infrastructure for our new society, but as Leibowitz argued, what was really being accomplished was the production of a class of competent technocrats, certainly not the pioneering activists for a society we were striving to bring into existence. The training succeeded as training, said Leibowitz, but not as education. It did not produce better human beings. Training for different careers in the guise of education toward pioneering values has done nothing to counter venality, avarice, stupidity, and base materialism. And in the meantime, other ideals, other ideologies have jostled in to fill the spiritual cultural vacuum created by our retreat.

Ben-Gurion's statism clashed head-on with our socialist philosophy. But the labor movement never resolved the inherent contradictions. Our new social philosophy was never redefined. No new ideologies with which we could come to grips with urgent social issues were ever formulated. Welfare statism and national insurance were seen as a natural continuation of socialism. Nationalization of means of production seemed irrelevant given the fact that the state had to play a major role in the economy for lack of private capital. National resources were distributed freely to entrepreneurs in order to encourage private initiative. The redistributive ethos—state intervention in the distribution of national income to enhance social equality—seemed to be redundant. Class struggle in a community of impoverished immigrants seemed absurd.

Bitzuism, the activist impulse to create material assets, to expand the state bureaucracy, replaced social vision. An entrepreneurial spirit not unlike neocapitalism—industrialization, technological progress, "a car for every worker"—was perceived as the new social message. But the old ethos with its symbols and high-flown rhetoric remained. Nostalgia for the blue shirt of the youth movement persisted, and people thought of themselves as socialist revolutionaries while speculating on the stock exchange. Kibbutz financial wizards gained and ultimately lost millions of dollars in attempting to make easy profits. Some were even caught embezzling public funds and sentenced to imprisonment. We could not extricate ourselves from the old ethos of *hagshama;* we had invested too much emotional and intellectual energy in it. But at the same time we sensed that it did not and could not supply answers to the new questions that confused us.

So we gave up social vision altogether and concentrated on creating physical facts. Our dream was translated into quantifiable units: so many new schools and factories opened, the expansion of commerce, the development of tourism. But the whole notion of raising man to a higher plane and creating a just society is forgotten, and nationalism has replaced socialism as the motivating force. We made a magnificent attempt to create new social frameworks for nurturing new and wholesome human relationships, but in the final analysis we have to admit that it achieved very little. People essentially stayed the same. And it is not even so demonstrable that an Israeli Jew is necessarily a great improvement on his Diaspora counterpart.

It could be that the people we derided and dismissed because of their lack of faith in our brand of massive social engineering and who persisted in seeing things in more modest proportions were really right. But we stuck to our gargantuan pretensions even though our field of activity had shrunk dramatically. It led us straight to elitism and ultimately to encapsulation and introversion.

Elitism was built into our concept of ourselves. Our parents had come here of their own volition and from ideological motivation. They were not driven here by persecution. All the others, those who fled from persecution, would have to be reeducated. We were a sect, but we did not want to remain only a sect. We wanted to assimilate the new immigrants from Iraq and North Africa—all those whom in our arrogance we termed *dor hamidbar,* "the generation of the wanderers in the desert."

To do credit to our intentions, however misguided, it must be said that we did not want to repel or exclude them. We wanted to assimilate them. We used to go to the *ma'abarot,* the immigrants' temporary housing projects in tents and huts, and run youth groups for them. We brought them to our kibbutz. We believed that in teaching them personal hygiene, educating them, teaching them how to behave like us, we were doing the right thing. We truly wanted nothing better than for them to embrace our way of life. We never dreamed that we were injuring their self-respect, inspiring pure hatred in them toward us and our kind. It was a genuine and sincere, if misguided, attempt to integrate them. But in the manner in which we were trying to do it, it was clearly impossible to achieve. We tried to make them over in our image, but our framework was wholly unsuited for them. It was militantly secular; it did not take into account their familial values, their religious traditions, or their urban culture.

They had not the vaguest understanding of our laboring ethos. As they saw it, people did not do manual labor out of choice. They did it because they could not afford to go into clerical jobs or business. They could not fathom why we set such store by the communal dining hall, the children's house. As for our socialist aspirations—certainly they had not the ghost of a conception of our mixture of socialist-anarchist antecedents, spiced with Buber and Marx.

We were not willing to compromise ourselves by relinquishing our pioneering character, and therefore were incapable of assimilating new immigrants. We wanted followers and converts—but only on our terms. Not that we did not reach out for them, but our two groups were light-years apart. What we did was emphatically not—as it is so often portrayed—a cynical attempt to harness these people to the needs of the cooperative sector as a mere population resource. It was a genuine, admirable, and even magnificent attempt that was undermined by its uncompromising standards and its total obliviousness to the nature of the people with whom we were dealing.

We were so self-centered that when we could not permeate society with our ideals, we put it down to the fact that we were "too good" for the world and we retired into capsules.

Part of our feeling of legitimacy in those early days arose from our commitment to creating the network of socialist cells on which the just society would be founded. But those who believed they were building the units of socialist society have retreated today into enclaves. It is analogous to Peter Berger's discussion of the major churches that once provided the guiding ethos of the Christian West. In many cases they have diminished into enclaves that preserve their internal structures intact, and provide the appearance and conviction in their members of ongoing normality and legitimacy—but within an enclosed environment that recruits individual members but has lost its leadership role.

In November 1982 the novelist Amos Oz stepped out of his kibbutz enclave and set out to see what was happening in his country. His account, *In the Land of Israel*, reads like a travel book. He discovered a bestiary of fabulous creatures: disaffected Moroccan youth whose hatred of Arabs is only rivaled by their hatred of Ashkenazim; West Bank settlers fired with the coming of the Messiah; megalomaniac, fascist farmers. Oz was no longer a member of a ruling elite but an explorer, somewhat similar to a Captain Cook. What is most appalling to him is the aggression he encountered. The immigrants of the fifties and their children, now grown to adulthood, rant about the arrogance and paternalism of the kibbutzim. Their complaints cannot be conveniently put down to a chip on the shoulder.

The burning sense of insult that Amos Oz encountered when he visited the new town of Beth Shemesh seems shocking and undeserved to many Israelis of my generation and background. But Kibbutz Hulda, where Amos Oz lives, lies a quarter of an hour's journey from Beth Shemesh. He left his ivory tower after "almost twenty years" to go among the people and found outrage and alienation, the worship of strange gods, exotic and repugnant forms of life rampant and flourishing. This is the net result of a superiority and elitism that eventually led to encapsulation and ultimately to a complete severance from reality—or, at any rate, from the way most people live. "Nice of you to come and see how we're getting on," the raw youth of Beth Shemesh say sardonically to the likes of Amos Oz. "And when can we come and see you in your kibbutz? to campaign for the Likud? swim in your pool? go out with your women?"

The kibbutzim were not planned as retirement communities for like-minded people. They were intended as regional clusters from which their members and activities would reach out to surrounding towns and villages. They still exist, they still possess vitality and enterprise, are the backbone of Israel's agriculture, run many important export enterprises and large industrial concerns, and still contribute disproportionately to the top ranks of the army despite the demoralization that has set in with the occupation of the West Bank and the Lebanon war. They are charming communities to visit with their well-kept gardens, shaded walks, and pleasant, well-designed communal areas. Visitors are usually captivated by the energetic, likable people and their radiantly healthy children. But the kibbutz population has been frozen for years at 4 percent of the general population and seems unlikely ever to exceed it. True, this low percentage has a great deal as well to do with the changing demands of an industrialized society where an ever larger percentage of people will be diverted from agriculture into urban centers and services. The kibbutz continues to be unique and interesting, and to contribute more than its share of outstanding leaders and creative people to the wider society, but as for being an elite capable of transforming that wider society, they have more or less abandoned that as a long-term goal.

It is easy to see from leafing through recent editions of the kibbutz quarterly *Shdemot* just how immured the kibbutz movement is in its enclaves. Though there is a serious attempt to come to terms with contemporary events like Lebanon and the West Bank, many of the same topics that were being written about fifteen and twenty years ago are still being churned out: the poor relations with development towns; the ethics of employing Arab labor; the need for family living arrangements and a move away from the children's house; the narrow scope for women on the kibbutz. Outside the fairly leisured approach to these issues in these peaceful enclaves, events whirl dizzyingly. Perhaps Amos Oz's voyage of discovery is an indication, however belated, that at last we are prepared to take seriously these different groups that have proliferated so alarmingly. Where he was before, while they were in their formative stages—where we *all* were before— is a different matter. What does matter is that in his book he grants them unedited hearing in order to pose the formidable challenge they represent.

Yet elitism persists. In the snapshots of fabulous beasts collected by Oz, one is missing: a snapshot of the dinosaur. His own environment, Kibbutz Hulda, is notably omitted. It is the only environment that ostensibly remained unaltered in its pristine purity. It is the norm. All the others are only deviations. In my circle of friends we frequently use expressions like, "We hold a passport of a country that doesn't exist," or, "The country has sidetracked."

One political expression of that elitist feeling is our perception of Menachem Begin and the Likud administrations. Much of our contempt for them rose from our conviction that "they" were not truly legitimate. They were usurpers, elected by "pickle-and-watermelon-stall owners in the marketplace" as the current offensive expression has it—not by "us." Their victory in elections was perceived by us as a terrible road accident, and Begin himself as an aberration. We never forgave Begin for sitting in the chair of Ben-Gurion and Golda Meir, and we anticipated avidly his stumbling. We knew that he, and not "us," represents Israel's proletariat, that 70 percent of all Oriental, underprivileged voters vote Likud, while 70 percent of all Ashkenazic, middle-class Israelis vote Labor. We understood that his victory was caused by the sense of collective insult, fury, and rage that these people nursed for a generation and that finally erupted. Rage against our patronizing attitude, our elitist behavior, our perception of ourselves as "*tout* Israel." We understood, but attributed it to ethnic characteristics, to lack of civic culture, to Begin's demagoguery. We were insulted by the lack of gratitude: such hatred after what we have done for them. We read each other's articles in the papers; we attend Peace Now rallies, meet "everybody," and joke how few "suntanned" people there are among us. There is always a poet or a writer present to eloquently express our feelings. We haven't changed—we are still beautiful, strong, the sons of light. The rallies of "the others," with the frenzied shouts of "Begin, King of Israel," the uncontrolled emotions, the occasional violence, are regarded by us as the "culture of the city squares."

We are aghast when we see how little impact our socialist and egalitarian ethos has had on public and community life, how ineffective we were in transmitting a legacy of civic concepts to the younger generation and the immigrants we absorbed. Yet it is too painful for us to admit to ourselves that we have no answers or solutions for the problems confronting us today. Our old ideology is still reflexive, instinctive, yet sustains us no longer. It became fossilized, and our vanguard elitism has degenerated into sheer snobbery. In bad conscience we co-opt Sephardim on "quotas" for ethnic representatives; we initiate "dialogues" with "Sephardic intellectuals." In our confusion we believe that by blurring the ideological differences between "us" and "them" we can gain legitimacy. Our principal consolation is in embracing the material assets we have created—"what there is"—and elevate it to the plane of ideology. Ketzaleh's eulogy supplies ample examples. But a more systematic expression of the admission of defeat can perhaps be found in Amos Oz's epilogue: "Perhaps we should have aimed for less. Perhaps there was a wild pretension here, beyond our capabilities, beyond human capabilities. [Perhaps we should] waive messianic salvation for the sake of small, gradual reforms, forego messianic fervor for the sake of prosaic sobriety. And perhaps the entirety of our story is not a story of blood and fire and salvation and consolation but rather a story of a halting attempt to recover from a severe illness. . . . Israelis," hopes Oz, "are gradually learning to hold on by their fingernails to what there is. And what is, at best, is the city of Ashdod." Ashdod, a new port city inhabited by some eighty thousand Israelis, half Sephardic, half Ashkenazic, a nondescript cluster of modern housing estates, a modern port, some industrial plants, "a city on a human scale is all we have that is our own." Not the kibbutz, not Jerusalem, not even Tel Aviv. Ashdod, "a pretty city and to my mind a good one, this Ashdod," says Amos Oz.

This expression of defeat or "prosaic sobriety," the identification of all ideologies as "a messiah complex," stands, however, in total contradiction to the universally cherished ethos of Zionism as a perpetual revolution. It contradicts the raison d'être of the State of Israel, expressed in religious terms as the "beginning of Redemption" and in secular terms by the Law of Return. Every Jew, no matter where he lives and no matter what his emotional attachment to Judaism or to Israel, is seen as a potential citizen of Israel. He is viewed as a person who ultimately will join us in the *moledet*. He is obligated to share in our common destiny, to owe an allegiance to *his* state, the Jewish state. Israel is a territorial base, a haven, a pied-à-terre: Ashdod, Jerusalem, and the kibbutzim are not meant to be habitats for their citizens but to millions of potential citizens that will come eventually because of persecution or because of ideological motivation. It is a perpetual, unrelenting endeavor for the "ingathering of the exiles" that will not cease until the last Jew comes to live in the *moledet.* The constant ideological challenge posed to every Jew is aliyah, immigration to Israel. This is the ultimate sign of identification with the Jewish People, an act of faith. The worst sign of desertion is emigration from Israel.

The fact that for a decade aliyah, rarely offset emigration is perceived as a temporary setback. The fact that persecuted Jews in the Soviet Union or in Iran choose to immigrate to the West and not to Israel is blamed on the lack of initiative of those responsible for aliyah, not on some fundamental flaw in Zionist ideology. "The continuity of the Zionist enterprise" is the fundamental credo of both the left and the right in Israel.

Therefore, "national vision," a sense of national purpose beyond "what there is," is a basic requirement in the political platforms of all political parties, and the lack of it is unpatriotic or "un-Zionist." Existential ideologies are no match to "messianic complexes" of either religious or secular varieties. They are illegitimate even in the eyes of those who formulate them, and find expression only within the context of poetic license.

The national objectives of Zionism, unlike other nationalist ideologies, were not realized when we attained independence. The Zionist ethos, its symbols and policies, the institutions created to sustain them, are viewed as relevant because the conditions and the needs that created them are perceived as basically unaltered: the state's very existence is threatened, it is still not fully developed, only less than a quarter of the Jewish people live in their land, anti-Semitism is rampant, the Messiah is late in coming.

The old paradigm seems therefore valid. And the calls to adapt the ideological framework to the changing reality are viewed as heresy. The growing uneasiness caused by a diffused sense of the inadequacy of the old ideology is viewed as confusion emanating from ineffective indoctrination. A more rational cause-and-effect perception of reality that seeks to discern among the multiplicity of interacting factors and trends, various outcomes and consequences both intended and unintended, is viewed as "existentialism." Mystic and eschatological interpretations of reality are hailed as "true Zionism" and are supported and disseminated by the state educational system. A new belief system has replaced the old, but because it draws on the old myths and symbols, this fundamental change is rarely discerned. Israelis perceive the change only in the concrete, party-political context.

The old ideology, secular and reality-oriented, demanding self-realization through small but incremental contributions to the creation of a free and just society, has ceased to be the dominant ideology. It is replaced by a mystic, monistic ideology that demands nothing except belonging to the "national camp" and voting Likud in the elections. The ideological ferment and vitality has been taken over by people fired not with the vision of creating a just society but by settling Greater Eretz Israel. The old pioneering élan is restored, and languishing institutions are revitalized to facilitate the integration of the territories.

The sons of the founding fathers, out of residual feelings of guilt for abandoning *hagshama*, out of their drift from the pioneering way of life and their immersion in middle-class, hedonistic culture, are either attracted to the "new Zionism" or mount an extremely radical critique against it. Not being able to extricate themselves from the concept of the perpetual Zionist revolution, they concentrate on the most repugnant aspects of the current Israeli situation: rampant chauvinism, xenophobia, ethnic and national discrimination, clerical influence, political malaise, economic and social instability.

Nearly always, however, this critique is devoid of any positive program, and is voiced by loose coalitions that seem to coalesce only around criticizing but are unable to agree on a positive platform. When out of bitterness and despair the critique becomes extreme, it usually provokes a violent counterreaction. The fact that the radical leftist groups are predominantly secular, Ashkenazic, and middle class provokes ethnic, chauvinistic, and religious outrage against "elitist, unpatriotic, and permissive excesses." Observers emphasize the similarity between the Israeli left and the Social Democrats and Liberals in the German Weimar Republic. It was the failing of the intellectual left in Germany that while fully aware of the depth of the political malaise, they were never able to mount an effective offensive. These intellectuals, instead of aspiring to be builders of a new society, were merely impotent critics and were unable to provide alternative methods of change.

The opposing camp offers a simple, attractive ideology that resembles, *in form*, the old Zionist ethos. The solutions, argues Gush Emunim, are at hand. There is no need to reform the unpalatable aspects of Israeli society; you just remove yourself to a new "unspoiled" environment like the frontier American pulling up stakes and moving further west. In the West Bank the young zealots of the fundamentalist "Block of the Faithful" create the cells of the new society that they believe will eventually give rise to a general regeneration of the whole society. The new society, which they see as implacably anti-Western and in command of an unimpeachable moral character, will, they believe, provide a viable alternative to secularism and hedonism.

The old banner of our *hagshama* is turned upside down. Buber's communal settlements, "the form that enabled the socialist ideal to penetrate into the national core," the utopian nuclei of a new and just society committed to manual labor and an agrarian way of life, are replaced by a new type of settlement: the *yishuv kehilati* of Gush Emunim. These semi-urban, commuting, half-open settlements are the main type of new settlement in the occupied territories. Although many of them are planned merely as dormitory suburbs of Israeli towns, they are accorded recognition as legitimate "pioneering settlements" by the World Zionist Organization, and enjoy the same status as the first kibbutzim such as Degania, established in 1910.

Our socialist ideals are replaced by intense fundamentalist, religious ideology. One may argue that both are messianic complexes, but at least we could argue that our socialist dream was rooted in some kind of concrete reality, that our dairy or poultry represented a small but incremental contribution to the creation of a better society. The carpenter's shop in a West Bank settlement is aimed at bringing the Messiah! Our nationalism was a secular, rational concept. "New Zionism" is messianic deliverance, which coincides with the extension of our borders to include the whole of biblical Eretz Israel, the ingathering of *all* the exiles, and the restoration of the Temple cult.

The content is totally different, but the form and appearance are not so different. It is not by accident that the fundamentalist settlers in the West Bank dress as we dressed forty years ago. The same army surplus fatigues, the same jargon, the same simple, sabralike, warm, nonchalant mannerisms— except for the yarmulke. The resemblance runs even deeper. In listening to Gush Emunim members, I detect the same sense of elitism, the same contempt for the petit-bourgeois flavor of urban life and the ravages of a consumer society that we felt.

Our rejection of the city was total. In our view, the city was a breeding ground for the worst forms of inequality. We abandoned the towns not in order to abandon the struggle to refashion society but in order to prepare ourselves for an eventual return. We returned as youth leaders and trained further activists, making, so we believed, small changes in the fabric of society. The creative aspects of urban culture could not counter our dismissal of the city and all its works. I recall the very sentiments aroused. When I was a member of Rosh Haniqra, I remember traveling on a Haifa bus and looking around at my fellow passengers with contempt and indifference—almost as lower forms of human life. Today, elitism is built into Gush Emunim's concept of itself. They regard ideals like the brotherhood of man with contempt, as the pitiful creations of the self-hating, self-doubting Jew. Their elitism and nonrepresentativeness bothers them even less than ours bothered us. Their perception of themselves as the forerunners of the Messiah underlies their sense of elitist mission, whereas ours had no significance beyond itself and its human, concrete dimension. But as far as elitist sentiments are concerned, we have much in common.

There is another intriguing comparison: the attitude toward the state. Our attitude to the state was ambivalent. We fought for the establishment of a Jewish state but viewed its institutions with extreme suspicion—a coercive factor that crushes all real spirit, induces materialism, and runs contrary to free, moral choice and voluntary action. The attitude of Gush Emunim is equally ambivalent. On the one hand, they sanctify the institutions of the state, viewing them as instrumental to accelerate the Redemption. On the other hand, they do not accept the secular authority of the elected government. The future of the occupied territories is not considered by them as a political issue but rather a divine one; therefore, it is divine laws that should be obeyed. Divine will is interpreted by Gush Emunim's religious leaders and supersedes the authority of the state. From opposite —humanistic versus messianic—perceptions, we both reject the Hegelian concept of the state as representing the absolute moral imperative.

Last winter I went to one of Gush Emunim's intellectual centers in Western Samaria to conduct a "dialogue." We all seem to have the same urge. Amos Oz went there in a desperate attempt to understand, to convince, to argue, as he puts it, "on matters of life and death, pure and simple."

Zvika is one of the leaders of the Gush. He is a veteran of numerous settlement attempts in the West Bank, legal and illegal; a roving ambassador of the Gush in Israel and abroad; a founder of an educational center whose application to become a "recognized school for higher education" is pending. It is an attractive structure, complete with its classrooms, an archaeological exhibit ("showing the Israelite settlement of Samaria in biblical times"), a library ("of books on Eretz Israel") and a secretariat ("to meet the enormous demand for lectures"). It is financed by various official Israeli agencies. During my visit I saw groups of Israeli soldiers sent by the army for seminars.

In his office Zvika was talking, or, rather, lecturing me, with the same inner conviction that reminded me of my own talks with my youth groups. I was interested in gathering facts and figures for my West Bank research project, but he was keen on convincing me. I listened to arguments essentially meant to persuade me that the Gush is the legitimate successor to the founding fathers, that in ten short years they have revitalized the Zionist enterprise. They bought land from the Arabs, reclaimed rocky hills, built settlements despite administrative and legal constraints, maintained excellent relations with the neighboring Arabs, created a powerful educational system that radiates influence on Israeli society and instills in thousands of Israeli youth the love for *moledet*. Zvika had not forgotten to use all the Zionist code words, to mention all the legendary names, to express concern for social justice and the "love of Israel," deploring divisiveness, laxity, "drifting from the sources." In short, an eloquent, concise course in Zionism for beginners.

During the lecture I felt a vague sense of déjà vu, but I could not recall what he had reminded me of. Suddenly it dawned on me: The White Russian Church in the Old City! Near the Church of the Holy Sepulchre in Jerusalem stands a pink rococo structure built by the czars of Russia in the mid-nineteenth century. After the Revolution, the émigré White Russian clergy fled the country and succeeded in keeping some of their holy places in Jerusalem despite attempts by the official Russian Pravoslav Church to displace them. When you enter the church you enter a time capsule. The offices of the archbishop are furnished with heavy, dark furniture from the turn of the century with chintz upholstery. Delicate lace curtains cover the windows. Oil paintings of Czar Nicholas, Czarina Alexandra, and various grand dukes hang on the walls. The imperial flag is displayed. Official Jerusalem knows that in the receptions given by the church on the occasion of the Old Russian national day one would be served beluga caviar. In the long corridors old Russian monks, dressed in black with long white beards, and nuns, formerly grand duchesses, move about. The conversations are always polite, civilized, not desperate. The White Russians in the pink church of St. Alexander know that they are in temporary exile, that they shall return to Moscow. For them the past, present, and future are fused together. Time is not a chronological, mechanical sequence; it is a countdown to their Redemption.

I had a clear insight into that different concept of time when visiting that strange environment. It repeated itself in the Gush Emunim center. Zvika's notion of time was similar. His perception of it is cyclical. Abiding by the Jewish imperative, "In every generation everyone is obliged to regard himself as though he himself had actually gone forth from Egypt," he honestly believes that he is one of Joshua's chieftains, a Second Temple zealot, and a second aliyah peer of Ben-Gurion. Jewish communal experience is timeless. All Jews must internalize past events as if they happened to them personally only yesterday. My father still feels the agony of the expulsion from Spain as if it happened to him personally and not five hundred years ago.

For Zvika, the chronological time, the progress of the clock, the changing reality is mechanical and meaningless. The only meaningful thing is the timeless experience of the Jewish people as expressed by the Prophet Samuel: "The strength [in Hebrew, Eternal One] of Israel will not lie" (I Samuel 15:29). The reality is but *hevlai mashiah*, the birth pangs of the Messiah, a period of agony preceding Redemption. Millions of Jews went to their deaths in the camps singing, "I believe with absolute faith in the coming of the Messiah and even if he tarries, eventually he will appear. I shall daily await him." It is an *a*historic philosophy of an *a*historic people. It sustained us for two thousand years and is so imbued in our psyche that it was not altered even when we made the profound leap from an ahistoric, dispersed, and powerless people to an historic, independent, and powerful nation.

Indeed, Zionism itself is perceived as rebellion against reality. It is successful precisely *because* it ignored reality and never succumbed to rational perceptions of reality that predicted its doom.

Faced with that perception of reality and of time, what could I tell Zvika? That they are bringing disaster upon all of us? To cite demographic figures, to describe political and sociological scenarios? To tell him that we live in a real world, that by creating a state of our own we have accepted willy-nilly some universal codes of behavior and become a concrete factor whose actions have concrete outcomes and consequences? That his countdown to Redemption may be the countdown of our demise? He would dismiss all that as "Hellenization," referring to the struggle of the ancient Jewish sages against Greek and Roman cultural influence, and meaning Western humanistic values and perceptions of reality. There was no point in a discourse on catechism. In my frustration I could only reply thus: "To whom do you think you are preaching? All the legendary Zionist personalities are my father's peers. I know your family. They were anti-Zionist Orthodox Jews in the ghetto in Jerusalem. They, in the twenties, considered my father an atheist anarchist who would by his deeds provoke the goyim and bring disaster upon them. You are a Johnny-come-lately who discovered pioneering in 1967. You sit in your cozy office guarded by the Israeli Defense Force, sequester land using the coercive power of a sovereign state and call it reclamation, build settlements with funds freely provided by government ministries. You honestly believe that you are continuing the deeds of the starving swamp reclaimers—or the builders of illegal tower and stockade settlements who were arrested by the British police. Your anachronism would be pathetic if it were not damned disastrous. It not only makes a mockery of all my cherished symbols, it absolutely undermines the very foundation of the Zionist ideology." Admittedly a totally useless outburst.

On my way back I recalled what Saul Friedlander said about the early pioneers: "You have to admit this about the Jewish pioneers of that time: they certainly had a way of looking at things which we consider naïve today. . . . But it must be said, in order to establish the historic truth—insofar as we can speak of truth—that the Zionists had a well-defined subjective will, but the objective results of their action did not tally with their primary intentions."

We have internalized our parents' hopes, their subjective will, but we have not been able to escape their contradictions. They sheltered us from them and from untidy reality by their glorious naïveté, by their integrity, and the power of their conviction. Their colossal achievements persuaded us that objective reality can be shaped by the sheer power of ideological commitment. We never examined whether that ideology could survive the passing of time and changing circumstances. It seemed to us everlasting. We perceived it as a comprehensive theory, not as it really was, a pragmatic, flexible, and evolving system. But at last we had to face the cruel confrontation between the primary intentions and the objective reality. When we tried to address our own exigencies with the old ideology, we found that our contradictions could not be reconciled by it any longer. Like spoiled children suddenly thrown out of their sheltered environment, we were caught unprepared. Paralyzed and frightened, suffering from acute cognitive dissonance, we withdrew and left the arena to those who were never bothered by the discrepancy between the primary intentions and the ensuing objective reality. These forces never shared our parents' hopes for a reconciliation of humanism and nationalism, Judaism and universalism. Indeed, they always treated them as confused, ambivalent, and self-doubting fools and believed in monistic, "absolute" values such as land, nation, power.

We watch in despair how our parents' sense of mission, their deeds, even their pragmatic tactics are usurped and twisted. The fossilized shell of the pioneering ideology, while keeping its brilliant exterior and attractive contours, is totally empty within and used to justify repugnant policies and immoral actions. Basic concepts, which under different circumstances were honorable and moral, have turned out to be sinister and reactionary.

All lofty social ideals are double-edged swords. All moral

stances possess an immoral option. Concepts formulated to cope with a given situation and proven successful tend to become absolute, eternal, good for all times. Under different circumstances, those same concepts may acquire contrary meaning. All Zionist ideals were shaped in the pre-state era. Their successful realization rendered them absolute and valid forever. The new meaning they acquired in the context of a sovereign state, a Jewish majority, a powerful army, dominion over another nation, did not do them any good.

Jewish elitist perceptions of the "chosen people" were crystallized against the background of humiliation, scorn, hate, and alienation in the Diaspora. Only the belief in his unique identity could sustain the Jew. "Pour out Thy fury upon the heathen [in Hebrew, *goyim*] that know Thee not, and upon the families that call not on Thy name: for they have eaten up Jacob and devoured him" (Jeremiah 10:25) we say on Passover eve and open the doors to watch for agents of the Inquisition. We are forbidden to drink wine touched by a gentile or bless his bread. How else could we have survived?

The selfsame precepts, transferred to a situation where the Jews are the majority, ruling another nation, interacting on an equal basis with the goyim, assume a sinister, domineering significance. *Ahavat Israel*, the love for Israel, the deep sense of affinity and of common destiny, the belief in *col Israel haverim* (all Israel are comrades) which sustained the dispersed Jews and gave them a measure of security, resulted in xenophobia—being increasingly perceived as synonymous with *sin'at hagoy* (hate for the goyim).

Anti-Semitism was perceived by the founders of Zionism as a cosmic, everlasting phenomenon. This basic condition of isolation and hatred was the result of the Jews' anomalous existence in the Diaspora and could not have been solved by Enlightenment and Emancipation: "Lo, the people shall dwell alone, and shall not be reckoned among the nations" (Numbers 23:9). Zionism, the creation of a Jewish collective on the ancestral land, normal and equal, was therefore perceived as the only viable solution to anti-Semitism.

Zionism believed that a sovereign Jewish state that would be accorded equal status in the international system would eliminate the hatred and victimization of the Jew. Israel, however, remained isolated, and since 1967 has become one of the pariah states in the international system. Israelis do not try to explain their isolation in rational terms such as opposition to their holding on to the occupied territories or international power politics. For them it is a recurrence of anti-Semitism directed now toward the Jewish *state* instead of toward *individual* Jewish communities in the Diaspora. This being the case, all criticism can be dismissed as anti-Semitism and unfavorable actions perceived as an added instance of persecution.

If Israel is destined to remain a state that "shall dwell alone" in a hostile world, then everything is perceived as a matter of sheer survival, and human and international rules are those of a zero-sum game. Israel can rely only on itself and on the Jewish people abroad and need not abide by acceptable international norms of behavior. Outrage against Israeli excesses, such as the systematic bombing of Beirut in 1982, is dismissed as an instance of traditional anti-Semitic bias. The Zionist ideal of the moral superiority of a Jewish state, *a light unto the goyim*, is replaced by a concept of the superior moral claim of Israel, justified by Jewish suffering.

The Zionist movement, and in particular the Labor-Zionist stream, was determined to prevent a rise of a colonial society in Palestine consisting of Jewish masters and Arab peons. They built a separate Jewish society with little or no interaction with the existing and developing Palestinian society. This dual system functioned side by side, and its components were separately stratified.

Opponents of the Zionist enterprise regarded the dual system as discriminatory and even racist. This accusation seems ridiculous considering the alternative, and ignores the main difference between Palestine under the Mandate and a colonial society. Here Jewish and Arab societies were *equally ranked* under the colonial administration. Neither had control or even access to the state enforcement instruments and could not rely on the government to act in its favor.

The dual system spread to all spheres of Zionist activity— homogeneous Jewish settlements and cities, separate economic sectors, underground army, separate political institutions, and an independent cultural system. Its amazing success was due to a large extent to Palestinian actions aimed at disrupting Arab interaction with the Jews, policies culminating in a three-year-long Arab boycott (1936–39) and armed revolt. The dual system, termed in Zionist history as the "phase of the embryo state," became a cornerstone of the Zionist ideology.

The establishment of a sovereign Jewish state did not alter the concept of the dual society. Zionist policies of separate development continued, resulting in a systematic discrimination of the Israeli Arab minority. However, the altered meaning of the old concept under new circumstances was revealed in full after 1967 in the occupied territories: instead of equally ranked ethnic-social systems, a status hierarchy of superior-subordinate groups was institutionalized. A separate but unequal principle is employed in all sectors enforced by the instruments of coercion of the state. These inequalities are explained away by the status of military occupation but are also hailed as progressive and liberal. They seem legitimate because they are perceived as a direct continuation of the pre-state policies and ideology, and are seen as "recognition of ethnic diversity which allows for separate and free development of the minority."

Our Zionist, liberal-socialist philosophy did not escape the fate of other great liberating ideologies. Its failure to adjust to changing realities enabled dark forces to usurp its revered symbols, now fossilized and anachronistic, and turn enlightened, moral, and progressive ideas into reactionary beliefs and immoral deeds.

The crunch came in 1967. The contradictions, ambivalence,

and conflicting values inherent in *moledet* and *hagshama* surfaced. They were tested against the reality of conquest and occupation, and were found wanting. I shall describe now how they failed to provide me, as a participant in the affairs of Jerusalem, with any clear guidelines. It is also time to introduce the elusive hero of my narrative, my Arab neighbor.

4

A Traitor and a Bridge

A traitor and a bridge are very much alike; both go over to the other side.

Rev. Dr. Ian K. Paisley

Muhammad was arrested on Saturday morning in mid-July 1983. My wife located me in Yusef's store, where I used to spend some Sabbath mornings, gossiping. She said Muhammad asked her to notify his wife, Amina. He was allowed only one telephone call. The investigator, a plainclothes policeman, said that my friend was detained on charges of sedition and contact with "a hostile organization," a euphemism for the Palestine Liberation Organization. I was flabbergasted, outraged at the preposterous charges, but the policeman, studying his papers, told us that the charges were based on a report of the Shin Bet (the secret police) and "are serious."

I demanded to see Muhammad, who was locked in an adjacent room. The policeman refused. I raised my voice so that my friend would hear I was there and know that he was not alone. I did not know then how alone he really was.

Seven years before, I had received a call from a hospital on the Mount of Olives advising me that Muhammad had suffered a severe shock caused by an allergic reaction to a drug, was pronounced clinically dead, revived, but was in critical condition. Being then in city government, I appropriated an intensive care ambulance and removed him to Hadassah Hospital, where he recovered. This time, in the investigation section, I could not help him escape his fate. He had to drink the full cup of sorrow.

During the summer of 1983 I reported every morning to courtroom Number 2 in the Russian compound. At the appointed hour Muhammad arrived from his detention cell, chained to his eight comrades. The room and the corridor were filled with scores of relatives, young and old, my neighbors from the same cluster of small stone houses perched on the slope of the valley of Hinnom, sons of this hard, cruel city—neighbors and enemies. We all stood up to the call of the clerk, and His Honor sat on the bench: a benign, burly, Arabic-speaking Sephardic Jew, a friend and neighbor of my father, the father of my eldest son's first sweetheart. For forty-four days police officers and experts for "Arab affairs" set forth the indictment: Muhammad and his comrades managed a neighborhood sports and medical-aid club. According to the prosecution the club served as a cover for hostile activities. The evidence submitted consisted of pictures of a Palestinian flag painted on an interior wall of the club, some Palestinian posters found lying folded in a corner, and handwritten essays calling for "struggle against Zionism." Later I learned that the police action was aimed at "warning the Arabs not to engage in communal activity that may be infiltrated by the PLO and indirectly financed by terrorist organizations."

The evidence was considered irrefutable even by the defense: Palestinian patriotic symbols, even the combination of the colors of the Palestinian flag, are "seditious materials" according to the Law for the Prevention of Terrorism. The defense tried only to prove that the defendants were not responsible personally or did not know about the flag, the posters, or the leaflets. The judge refused repeated pleas for the release of the defendants on bail because of the "severity of the charges."

At the end of each session, Muhammad and his comrades were escorted, chained, to their dark, filthy cell.

At first I did not realize the full magnitude of Muhammad's predicament. One evening, in the second week of the trial, he called me at night from a public phone in an emergency ward. He had faked an attack of his kidney disease, was taken to a hospital, and managed to make the call. "My comrades tried twice to stab me," he said. "They claim that I am an informer. If you will not separate me from them, I'll be dead! Promise me to do something, or I won't tell the doctor about my allergy and will die right away. It is better than waiting for the knife in the darkness of the cell."

Muhammad was moved to solitary confinement for his protection, which confirmed the suspicion of his comrades. His family, wife, and eleven children were ostracized, threatened, and molested; members of the family came from their village to protect them. My friend was faced with a double charge: during the day, of being a Palestinian terrorist; during the night, of being an Israeli *jasus* (informer and spy). This is the place to tell that Muhammad was for many years my deputy, and later the highest-ranking Arab official in the city government, with an independent position and discretionary funds.

Upon his arrest the city fired him, although it provided him with funds to conduct his defense. Muhammad was found guilty and sent to prison. The judge refused to grant him a postponement, so his appeal was heard after he had served his term in full. The court of appeals acquitted him in a session that lasted all of ten minutes.

My friend, brokenhearted, suffering from acute paranoia, needed a long period of convalescence. Then he opened a grocery store on the border of the Armenian and the Jewish quarters. He refused to return to his job. "The only thing I am ready to do with the Jews," he said, "is to sell them *laban* [buttermilk]." He became a pious Muslim, observing the fast of Ramadan, refraining from drinking alcohol, praying five times a day. After the trial I met an Arab journalist in the street. "Don't think that we are upset about Muhammad," he told me. "On the contrary, it taught our people a good lesson —what happens to those who work for you: when you need us, you use us, then—you simply dispose of us."

I met Muhammad in 1968, a few months after the 1967 war. Our lives became interwoven, our relationship—professional, personal, and emotional—that of close brothers. He was a *dod* (uncle) to my little children, I an *a'am* (uncle from the father's side) to his. We were a strange couple. Muhammad, a native of a small hamlet on the western slopes of Mount Hebron, was a 1948 refugee. His family moved during the war to a larger village and lost their land, which remained beyond the armistice line, in Israel. Like many village youth, he gravitated to the big city, studied in the refugee vocational school, traveled in the Arab world, then settled down in Jerusalem. Through family connections he got a job in the Arab municipality, then built himself a small house and planted fruit trees. I never asked him about his political views or about his involvement in Palestinian activities in Jordan, but I had no doubt about his proud Palestinian nationalist stances.

I asked Muhammad if he was ready to work with me. He asked if he would be called upon to participate in eviction of Arabs or to assist in land expropriation. I replied that he would not be asked to do anything that he considered in conflict with his convictions. At that time I was naïve enough to believe that a Palestinian and a Zionist could collaborate in building a bridge over the chasm dividing our respective communities in Jerusalem. It took both of us some time and much agony to realize what it was all about.

When on June 28, 1967, the mayor of Jerusalem, Teddy Kollek, appointed me administrator for "the eastern sector" (as the metropolitan area annexed to Israel was called in those days), I was totally ignorant of all matters pertaining to "the Arabs." This is a shocking statement coming from a native Jerusalemite who had lived his whole life in the city.

I lived with Arabs all my life, of course. Our neighbors on Gaza Road were Arabs, my father's Arab friends came to the house, I studied Arabic in primary school, and after forty years still remember the first Arabic lesson, which all my generation knows by heart: *Bayn Birzeit wa-'Atara fi qabr wali mash-hur* ("Between Birzeit and Atara there is a tomb of a revered holy man").

The memories of the first months of the 1947–48 war were still fresh: the shooting, the flight of our neighbors, the looting of the Arab neighborhoods, the shelling of Jerusalem, the siege, my father's injury. And after the armistice, the incidents along the fortified borderline dividing the city, the "infiltrators" or *fedayeen* attacks on isolated homes, the retaliations of the Israeli Army, the Bedouins I met in my hikes in the Negev, the relations I had with "Israeli Arabs" in Nazareth as a tourist guide. A life of encounters, proximity, interaction—yet remote, extraneous, alienated. As if I were watching them through an opaque glass wall. You see familiar human forms, but you don't relate to them; they have three-dimensional substance, yet they are meaningless. Their three-dimensional substance is severed from mine; I do not exist in theirs, nor do they in mine. There is a dramatic expression of that feeling, composed, ironically, a few weeks before the 1967 war. A ballad, "Jerusalem of Gold," written by songwriter Naomi Shemer—which became, in an altered form, the hymn of united Jerusalem—relates: "How the cisterns have dried up! The marketplace is empty and no one visits the Temple Mount in the Old City." The writer was referring to the Arab part of the divided city. What she meant was that if there are no Jews in the marketplace, it is empty; and if no Jews visit the Temple Mount, then no one visits at all. The tens of thousands of Arabs who filled the marketplace and the Temple Mount did not exist. One might think that those lines could have been written only in the context of the hermetically sealed wall that divided Jews and Arabs during the nineteen years of Jerusalem's partition. But the dichotomy existed before the partition, and persisted later.

One method of measuring the ethnic alienation is by looking at the pattern of segregated communities that characterized Jerusalem. In pre-1948 Jerusalem, twenty-six neighborhoods were homogeneous—Jewish or Arab. Only eight were mixed to a certain extent, but even in those there was enough of an ethnic majority to establish a distinct character. The mixed areas were situated mainly in and around the shopping and business district, but even there, the clientele of the Jewish, Muslim, and Christian shops was usually segregated. In what is perceived as "the good old days" of Jerusalem under the Palestine Mandate, 90 percent of the Jews and 90 percent of the Arabs lived in entirely homogeneous neighborhoods. It goes without saying that the school system, cultural life, and social networks were separated. Earlier on, I alluded briefly to the dual society that characterized Palestine under the Mandate. The spatial segregation of Jews and Arabs in a heterogeneous city such as Jerusalem illustrates the dual system even more dramatically than, for example, the separation of Jewish Tel Aviv from Arab Jaffa. Tel Aviv and Jaffa were almost totally segregated large urban areas. Here, the patchwork of alienated islands consisted of small clusters of ethnically homogeneous houses in close proximity. The physical contact was unavoidable, yet remote and adversarial.

I lived in the southwestern Jewish section of Rehavia, on the edge of the city, adjacent to the modern Arab neighborhoods of Katamon and Talbiya. Our neighborhood was no different in physical appearance from the Arab neighborhoods. Both were inhabited by middle-class, relatively affluent families. The gardens were well tended, the streets wide and clean, even the way people dressed was quite similar. Yet I went to a Hebrew school in Beit Hakerem, and my neighbors went to the Catholic school Terra Sancta. I ate eggs bought from a Jewish vendor, played with Jewish kids, observed Jewish religious and national holidays, and my father belonged to the Haganah—the underground Jewish army. The Arab neighbors conducted their economic, social, and cultural lives in a totally separated environment. We lived in different worlds.

Admittedly there were social, economic, and political contacts across the ethnic divide. Jews and Arabs worked in the same municipal offices, in the government, in construction. They met on neutral ground such as the lobby of the King David Hotel or at garden parties given by the high commissioner. There are scores of nostalgic accounts of a cosmopolitan pre-1948 Levantine Jerusalem that try to evoke the atmosphere of Alexandria as depicted by Lawrence Durrell. These accounts are probably exaggerated, but even if accurate, they describe an atmosphere that was limited to the upper crust of Jewish, Arab, and British society, and did not affect the masses on both sides. For the average Jew or Arab, the alienation was almost total.

Edward Said, in his book *The Question of Palestine*, refers to Jewish spatially segregated areas as "little Europes," and depicts Jewish life in them as "life in an enclave many physical and cultural miles from Europe, in the midst of hostile and uncomprehending natives." For him the fact that "they lived on Jewish bread raised on Jewish soil that was protected by Jewish rifles" is the outcome of a "ruthless doctrine" based on exclusion "deliberately shutting out the natives" similar in fashion to apartheid. All this is a gross distortion. I don't recall that my life-style was more "European" than my Arab neighbors in Katamon, that segregation was forced upon the Arabs, that any of them ever wanted to live in a Jewish neighborhood and were refused, or vice versa. Moreover, if there is one single factor that determined spatial segregation, it was Arab violence. Studies show how the pattern of settlement in Jerusalem closely followed the fluctuation of security conditions. Before the Arab riots of 1929 there were many heterogeneous neighborhoods in the city. Their number shrank because the Jewish inhabitants fled to Jewish areas. Segregation became almost total as a result of the Arab riots of 1936–39. Total severance of economic ties between the two communities occurred due to a general Arab boycott of the Jewish sector. Said complains that the importance of Tel Aviv as a Jewish center "derives in great measure from its having neutralized the adjacent (and much older) Arab town of

Jaffa," hinting at a deliberate, sinister attempt to outstrip and eventually destroy Arab Jaffa. What he fails to mention is that the greatest boost to Tel Aviv as a commercial center came as a result of Arab violence, which culminated in the total closure of the port of Jaffa, forcing the Jews to build their own port in Tel Aviv. Said may think that Arab violence and commercial boycott were justified as being defensive, but he cannot ignore their consequences and blame the dual society only on the Jews.

The dual system prevailing in Palestine under the British Mandate was an outcome of the communal strife, not its cause. Segmentation of ethnically heterogeneous cities is the spatial expression of inherent conflicting conditions that characterize plural societies. Segregation is a mechanism for coping with physical threat, a device to preserve group identity from alien cultural influences and to conserve cultural heritage and life-style. Segregated neighborhoods were built by Jews and Arabs voluntarily, and separation was caused by mutual exclusion, not unilaterally by a racist Jewish "doctrine." Edward Said may think that I had no right to be born in Rehavia, but to insinuate that my Jewish capsule there was exclusionary, colonialist, or racist is biased to say the least.

The fact that both Jews and Arabs share a responsibility for erecting the opaque glass wall between them is indeed a very poor consolation. Segregation was an inevitable outcome of the communal strife, but it also reinforced it. The defense mechanism of clustering around your own kind was a natural reaction, but it was also rooted in the fundamental perception of both sides of themselves and of the "other side"—of themselves as a besieged and threatened group, and of the other side as cruel, ruthless, and demonic. Dichotomy was reinforced by stereotypes disseminated through the educational system. The result was that both Jews and Arabs developed mutual and symmetrical exclusionary attitudes. Both sides viewed their adversary as an extraneous factor, illegitimate and externally generated. The Palestinians always viewed the Zionists as white-settler colonists, totally dependent on the

British, a nonviable artificial society bound to disappear. Said observes: "Zionism, [the Palestinians] said, was foreign colonialism—and it was doomed to die of its various theoretical weaknesses. They have not understood the Zionist challenge as a policy of detail, of institutions, of organizations." In other words, the Palestinians did not perceive us as a formidable, viable, and independent force. They underestimated us until it was too late. The "Zionist question" seemed to them less important than the "British Mandate question," and therefore they directed their political and later their armed struggle primarily against the British. The Zionists on their part ignored the "Palestinian question," viewing them as an external constraint, as noncohesive, primitive gangs of murderers incapable of forming a national movement. The "Arab population" of Palestine was perceived as an offshoot of the Arab world, not as an internally generated and independent factor. If the other side is underestimated or ignored, and manipulated by external forces, there is no point in trying to relate to it. If the other side is perceived as a demonic force set to destroy and annihilate—if the showdown seems inevitable—then the use of force is the only option.

Historians and politicians have poured out oceans of ink describing earlier phases of the Zionist-Palestinian encounter: lamenting faded opportunities for reconciliation; blaming Jews, Arabs, and British for extremism, intransigence, duplicity; pondering moral dilemmas of absolute and relative rights; questioning the inevitability of the bloody conflict. All these seemed to us, the generation born in Rehavia and in Katamon in the mid-thirties, totally irrelevant. All observers had agreed that at that time, the conflict had already passed the point of no return, and both sides were moving irrevocably and consciously toward total confrontation. The Palestinians had endorsed the principle of an all-out "armed struggle" and launched the "Arab revolt," a tremendous effort to overthrow the British Mandate and destroy the Zionist enterprise that lasted three years (1936–39). Faced with such a challenge, even the most moderate and conciliatory Zionists understood

that "we are doomed to live in a state of permanent belliger-
ency with the Arabs, and there is no way to avoid bloody
sacrifices; this may not be a desirable state of affairs, but such
is reality." These words were written by no other than Arthur
Ruppin, founder of Brith Shalom, the most moderate group
in the Zionist movement.

This was the mood even in moderate Rehavia, where in the
thirties many German Jews found refuge from Hitler, where
the highest per capita ratio of professors and musicians in the
world existed, and where Arthur Ruppin and most members
of Brith Shalom lived. This was also the mood in nearby Talbiya and Katamon, where peace-loving Palestinians developed their own modern, progressive educational system,
abhorred the fiery demagogues, but were unable to stay
aloof.

The violence and hostility had temporarily submerged. The
Arab revolt was crushed, and Palestine was engulfed in the
Second World War. The Jewish community had other worries:
the German Afrika Corps was at the gates of Alexandria, and
we prepared for a new Massada. We began to hear about the
extermination camps. After the war, we perceived the British
colonialists as our major enemy and forgot the Palestinians.
Yet alienation and exclusionary attitudes persisted and were
even exacerbated. The defeat of the Palestinians in 1938–39
seemingly confirmed our perception of the Arabs as a divided,
weak, and externally generated force. When the neighboring
Arab states had to interfere on behalf of the defeated Palestinians in 1939 and took over their cause, we felt that we were
justified in ignoring them. The 1948 war and its aftermath
reinforced our perceptions. Some of the fiercest battles between Jews and Arabs took place during the civil-war phase
prior to the establishment of Israel and the invasion of the
armies of the neighboring Arab countries; the battles of Qastal, Katamon, Bab-al-Wad, and others fought with the Palestinians in early 1948 are enshrined in the Israeli national
myth. Yet the War of Independence is perceived as a war of
the infant Jewish state against the invading armies of five

Arab states. The earlier, tougher, and vicious phase of communal rioting, shooting in the streets, flight of civilians, occupation of Arab neighborhoods, towns, and villages, pillage, and other incidents typical of civil war were erased from the Israeli collective memory.

We wanted to forget that phase because it reminded us that there was a Palestinian community with which we shared our cities and our land, a community that bitterly fought for what it believed had been its national objectives but which had been utterly defeated. Their total collapse, and the exodus of hundreds of thousands from the areas under our control, made us an ethnically homogeneous society. The "Palestinian question," we felt, had been eliminated by the disappearance of the Palestinians from our midst. Conceptual exclusion became a reality, and we could finally complete the process of externalization as objective reality caught up with the perceived reality. The Palestinians became "refugees" or "infiltrators," and the conflict became an Israeli-Arab conflict, a conflict between sovereign states. The opaque glass wall separating Rehavia from Katamon was replaced by barbed wire and minefields along the armistice line.

The Palestinians and other Arabs assisted us in rephrasing the problem. The incorporation of the nonoccupied parts of Palestine by the neighboring countries confirmed our view that the Palestinians were not an independent subject, but rather an object under full control of the Arab states. Even Palestinian perceptions of themselves pointed to the same direction. In the pan-Arab, Nasserite era, Palestinian activists put all their energies into supporting pan-Arab and antiimperialist movements. As Yehoshaphat Harkavi observed, "To view [the Palestinian problem] in the narrow framework of Palestinians versus Israel was stigmatized as antinationalist." The antiimperialist struggle was foremost in their mind. Like us, they clung to their old perceptions viewing the "Zionist entity" as a neocolonial, nonviable phenomenon relying for its sheer survival on imperialist power. They hated and despised us in a mixture of demonic and anti-Semitic stereotypes that reinforced our own demonic, invidious perceptions of the Arabs and our fear and contempt for them.

Our perception of the "Palestinian problem" affected our attitude toward the remaining Arab population. The sizable Arab minority inside Israel was ignored. It was perceived only in the context of "the conflict," viewed as a nonassimilating and nonassimilable alien group at best, a "fifth column" at worst. Their condition under military government, the massive land expropriations, the deliberate policies of discrimination were not perceived by most of us (including liberal, progressive groups) as issues to be concerned with because we viewed them as political and security problems. The Arab minority was outside the pale of Israeli society, a secondary, extraneous element in a homogeneous Jewish nation-state, a mere symptom of the overall conflict.

"Arab affairs" were entrusted to the capable and professional hands of "Arabists," experts for Arab affairs. Governors, advisers, correspondents, and Oriental scholars had monopolized the treatment of internal and external "Arab matters." Only they could interpret and represent them because they were acquainted with the "Arab mentality." Arab attitudes, sociology, even demography were not subjects that could be studied through "normal" behavioral sciences or by the "uninitiated." In his work *Orientalism*, Edward Said describes the phenomenon and quotes Disraeli, who said that Arabism (or Orientalism) "is a career in which one could remake and restore, not only the Orient, but also oneself." "Arab experts" carved themselves good, influential, and lucrative careers and guarded them with great zeal. The majority, myself included, pursued other careers. We couldn't care less about an issue that seemed to us an open-and-shut case. Not surprisingly, I wrote in 1967 that "my knowledge of the Arabs derived from my studies of the Crusader period and came to an end in 1291." The only meaningful Arab hero, for me, was Saladin (who, incidentally, was a Kurd).

Equipped with this knowledge, and with such perceptions,

I moved to East Jerusalem and opened an office in the al-Habash building off the main street named after my twelfth-century Arab hero, Salah-ad-Din. As it turned out, my ignorance of all "Arab matters" was actually an advantage. I was free of the "Arabist" grid of reference. I could absorb and internalize primary impressions without the burden of stereotyped images, the legacy of professional "Arabists." I could also act according to what I believed was correct, just, and professionally efficient without relying on conclusions drawn from "experience in dealing with the Arabs." Alas, not for long.

I was not alone. I found myself in the company of military administrators brought to the West Bank by Moshe Dayan. Dayan, the defense minister who was the supreme ruler of the occupied territories, loathed the policies of the military governors who since 1948 had controlled the Israeli Arab community, interfered in their internal affairs, restricted their movements, and harassed them. He refused to allow them to extend their jurisdiction to the territories. Instead he appointed regular and reserve combat officers free from the old tradition and directed them to establish good civilian government without trying to interpose an Israeli administration. Although tough, he believed in an honest dialogue with the Palestinian leadership in the West Bank. Although Jerusalem was considered, after June 28, 1967, to be part of Israel, the influence of Dayan and his military lieutenants remained decisive there. Naturally, the "experts" for "Arab affairs" were not prepared to give in without fighting back; East Jerusalem was too important to be handed over to the ignorant. We won some battles but lost others. We succeeded in frustrating repeated attempts of the "prime minister's adviser for Arab affairs"—the coordinator of government activities in the Israeli-Arab sector—to open an office in East Jerusalem; we succeeded in blocking the Ministry of Religion from censoring Friday sermons delivered in al-Aqsa Mosque; we cooperated in restoring the original school textbooks, expurgated by the director of Arab education for being "seditious." We returned property declared as "absentee property" to its owners. We could not stop expulsions, house demolitions, and expropriations, but on the whole we were a strong coalition of security officers and civilian bureaucrats who tried to implement liberal, professional policies despite pressures to apply "tougher" treatment. The common denominator was not ideological, it was pragmatic: heavy-handed enforcement breeds resentment, which encourages disobedience, which in turn necessitates even harsher measures. It's a vicious circle.

At first, all was quite straightforward. We were the first on the scene, we enjoyed the powerful backing of Moshe Dayan and of Mayor Teddy Kollek. All the others were busy establishing physical and symbolic facts of Israeli sovereignty at the Western Wall, on the Mount of Olives, in the Jewish Quarter. The key, in the eyes of most Israelis, was the creation of physical facts. The unification of Jerusalem was perceived as the incorporation of space: it was the land that was liberated. The human beings who happened to squat on it were not consulted on the revolutionary change in their lives. That goes without saying, but it is more interesting to note that they were not even notified officially about the annexation. The only official notice posted on a few walls was a poster signed by the Ministry of Finance concerning the obligation to change Jordanian dinars into Israeli lira, which began: "Whereas by the law [of annexation] Israeli jurisdiction applies to the area described below . . ."

Israeli actions in Jerusalem were guided by the profound feelings aroused by the return to the Wall and the Temple Mount, described elsewhere. It seems almost superfluous to describe the centrality of Jerusalem in the eyes of the Israelis. When the problem of Jerusalem was discussed in a special session of the General Assembly of the United Nations in July 1967, Abba Eban said:

> This is a concept which lies beyond and above, before and after all political and secular considerations. The eternal link between

Israel and Jerusalem [is] a link more ancient, more potent and more passionate than any other link between any people and any place.

Beginning with the return to Zion from the Babylonian Exile and the construction of the Second Temple, the whole city became an integral extension of the Temple, *the* holy place, the only one, in fact, of the Jewish religion. The half-shekel levy paid by every Jewish man in Eretz Israel and in the Diaspora for the Temple was also used to maintain "the aqueduct and the walls of the city and its towers and all the needs of the city." After the destruction of the Second Temple, longings intensified for "heavenly Jerusalem"; they served as a substitute for the redemption of "earthly Jerusalem." However, the rebuilding of "earthly Jerusalem" was not seen as a divine task but rather as a human possibility. "Heavenly Jerusalem," according to the sages of the Talmud, will always remain in its place, whereas the earthly city will be rebuilt and made firm and will aspire to be reunited with its heavenly counterpart. The reconstruction of Jerusalem was the essence of Jewish aspirations for two thousand years. The oath never to forget the destroyed city and the promise of "next year in Jerusalem" served as a banner to unify the Jewish Diaspora everywhere. It was not by chance that the leaders of the Jewish national liberation movement decided to call it by its other biblical name, Zion.

The Arabs were expected to emulate Israeli sentiments and accept the annexation peacefully. Perhaps they could not share the emotional experience of a reunited Jerusalem, but they must be tired of war, or at least understand that they have no choice. So they should better enjoy it and benefit from living in a modern welfare state, with running water and reliable electricity. On the eve of annexation a distinguished poet and political commentator wrote: "Tomorrow it shall become clear to all that most of the Arab citizens of Jerusalem wish to see the city united and the capital of Israel." The euphoria accompanying the realization of the dream of liberating the old city, combined with the profound ethnocentrist feelings aroused by the victory, utterly blurred reality.

The Arabs did nothing to destroy Israeli illusions; they suffered from a profound shock. The defeat and occupation were blows that descended on them with a force that is hard to overestimate. They were convinced that the Jews would put them on trucks and send them across the Jordan. Feelings of relief overcame them when they discovered that no one was going to harm them. The shock that had struck the Arabs numb contributed to the Israeli optimistic belief that annexation and peace were compatible. Subjective reality continued to sift objective reality even when the Palestinians who overcame their shock began to express their true feelings. At first the Israelis viewed Arab resistance as incitement stirred by a frustrated minority of leaders deprived of their position of power by the unification.

The Israelis believed that the masses were apolitical, pleased with the material benefits brought about by the annexation but easily incited to violence and disturbances. Clichés of the past were revived. The old perception of the Arabs as a primitive, docile community provoked by corrupt and fanatic leaders to kill and rob Jews determined Israeli reaction. Arab violence and strikes were seen as a repetition of the riots of 1929 or 1936, when defenseless Jews were massacred. These were the initial reactions. But when general strikes and mass demonstrations showed the Israelis that the Palestinians unanimously rejected the annexation, even the most naïve could no longer continue to indulge in pipe dreams: the national conflict after the unification of the city was more intense than prior to it.

Some Israelis realized the incompatibility of the positions of the two parties and perceived the conflict as one that only one side could win. Convinced from both a national and a moral point of view that Israel's claim to Jerusalem was far superior, to that of the Arabs, its implementation was not a subject for discussion. There was no room for the consideration of Arab demands, for these were perceived as attacks on the very existence of the State of Israel. Even simple civilian matters did not have to be treated on their merits because they were mere excuses meant to embarrass the authorities. Innocent Palestinian acts such as a shopkeeper's refusal to add a Hebrew inscription to his sign were depicted as hostile acts and as incitement against the unification of the city. Compromise was perceived as weakness, and any action except "full implementation of Israeli sovereignty" was seen as bordering on treason. Only an iron fist could dispel Arab hopes for change.

Some Israelis held more ambivalent positions. Their liberal philosophy clashed with their ethnocentrist sentiments. They could not ignore the fact that Israeli policies were implemented at the expense of the Palestinians, and that their status as conquerors conflicted with their self-image as peace-loving humanists. Yet they identified with basic Israeli national objectives. They overcame the ambivalence by using a number of mental devices. First, they tried to discount the symmetry of the two opposing claims by playing down Palestinian emotional ties: for the Jews, Jerusalem is the one and only holy city, while the Arabs place it third in their scale of sanctity. Second, they invoked democratic principles of majority rule: Arabs cannot demand self-determination because since the mid-nineteenth century there had always been a Jewish majority in Jerusalem. The Jewish majority of united Jerusalem has an unassailable right to decide on the future of the city by virtue of constituting a democratic majority.

Then there was the perception of the conflict as nonpolitical —whether economic, social, religious, or emotional. Unification was justified because it brought material benefits. Within a short time, economic improvements would moderate nationalistic aspirations. Nationalism is not so important to the Arabs anyway; Arabs should be identified according to religious affiliation as Muslims and Christians. Satisfaction of religious requirements would put an end to the conflict. Community action, communal get-togethers, sports activities, and the teaching of Hebrew and Arabic will do the trick. There was a strong paternalistic, condescending sentiment here: Arab hatred for Jews is rooted in their inferior cultural values and their poor economic state. If they were to acquire Western cultural values, hatred would diminish. Improved economic conditions would lead to the emergence of a new generation of Arabs who would work for a peaceful settlement based on the absolute sovereignty of Israel in Jerusalem. All these perceptions were based on self-delusion and emanated from the psychological inability to realize the centrality of Jerusalem for the Arabs.

The deep emotional attachment to and the desire to preserve the Arab nature of the holy city totally ruled out a possibility that Arabs would accept, in any manner or circumstance, the annexation of Jerusalem to Israel. But Israelis believed that the strength of Arab attachment for their city rests on the assessments of others. They simply excluded all other emotional bonds.

It is not easy to define the place of Jerusalem in Muslim consciousness throughout the history of Islam. The attitude of Islam toward Jerusalem was not unequivocal throughout the generations. Ever since its birth, Islam has acknowledged a degree of holiness to the site of the Temple: *Bayt al Maqdis.* However, the ascendancy of Jerusalem in the hierarchy of holiness was accompanied by difficulties and serious controversies. Those controversies were resolved after the conquest of the Crusaders. The propaganda promulgated by the Muslim rulers for a jihad against the infidels established the holiness of Jerusalem in the consciousness of the Muslims of Iraq, Syria, Palestine, and Egypt. The victory of Saladin and the conquest of Jerusalem confirmed the city's status as a holy place, and its name was connected in people's minds with Mecca and Medina.

As always, yearning for the lost beloved produced poetic expressions. Just like the Jewish exiles by the rivers of Babylon, who wept when they remembered Zion, Muslims sang the praises of the holy city when it was conquered by the Crusaders. A literary genre, the *Fadail al-Quds*, developed describing the virtues of Jerusalem and calling for its deliverance. Muslim writers, especially native Jerusalemites, depicted Jerusalem as the "most illustrious of cities, the pleasantest of places, the finest city, the one that unites the advantages of this world and those of the next." "Verily," said al-Mukaddasi in the eleventh century, "Mecca and Medina have their superiority by reason of the Kaaba and the Prophet . . . but in truth, on the day of Judgment both cities will come to Jerusalem, and the excellencies of them all will be united. And as for Jerusalem being the most spacious of cities; why, since all created things are to assemble there, what place on earth can be more extensive than this."

The emotional attachment of the Palestinian Arabs to Jerusalem is more complex and profound than that expressed in the general Muslim attitude. Natives of the land and those born in Jerusalem are linked to it spiritually and religiously more than to any other place. In their general spiritual experience, their emotional attachment to Jerusalem is naturally stronger than it is to Mecca. Here there are special rituals connected to the holy places. Because of the particular history of the land, those very places dear to the Jews are also most revered by the Palestinian Arabs.

The Israeli occupation in 1967 produced the same reaction as after the Crusader occupation in 1099. The fear of losing *Arab* Jerusalem was expressed in different ways. Copper etchings and wood engravings depicting the Dome of the Rock began to appear in Arab homes in Jerusalem, in the West Bank, and in Arab countries. Poets wrote laments. Fadwa Tuqan wrote: "God of the hills of Jerusalem, from the well of agonies, from the depth of the night, from the heart of laments, Jerusalem's outcry rises up to you; in Your compassion, do not pile on the agony." A song on Jerusalem and its suffering "under the foot of the conqueror," titled *"Zahrat al Madaen"* ("The Flower of Cities"), was broadcast frequently throughout the Middle East.

The knowledge of Muslim reaction to the Crusaders made

me aware of the similarity of Arab reaction to the second loss of Jerusalem, and in a curious way also sensitized me to their emotional suffering. I felt it keenly when I saw al-Aqsa Mosque on fire.

On Thursday, August 21, 1969, a mentally disturbed Australian tourist set fire to al-Aqsa Mosque on the Temple Mount. When I arrived with the fire brigade, the flames had already enveloped the interior. My first question was: "What happened to the *minbar* [pulpit]?" When I heard that it was totally burned, I realized the depth of the tragedy. The pulpit that went up in flames that day had been placed there on October 9, 1187, when Saladin offered his prayers on the first Friday after he purified the Temple Mount following the conquest of Jerusalem from the Crusaders. The pulpit was constructed twenty years earlier in Aleppo by command of Sultan Nur-a-Din, to be set in al-Aqsa after its liberation. I knew the profound symbolic significance of that *minbar* and the meaning of its destruction. In my ears, as in the ears of the weeping Muslims, rang the famous sermon delivered from the pulpit nine hundred years earlier: "O men! Rejoice at good tidings! God . . . hath helpeth you to bring back the strayed camel [Jerusalem] from misguided hands and restore it to the fold of Islam." I, a non-Muslim infidel and a hated occupier, stood there with tears in my eyes, overwhelmed with grief. Some time ago an Arab friend residing abroad visited Jerusalem. When we met, he told me that he went to pray in al-Aqsa. "But you are not an observant Muslim," I said. "Yes," he replied, "I haven't prayed since I was a child. But I felt I must pray at al-Aqsa because it is occupied, contested." He reminded me of another Arab-Syrian gentleman, Usamah Ibn Munqidh, Prince of Shaizar, who visited Jerusalem frequently when the city was occupied by the Crusaders: "Whenever I visited Jerusalem," tells Usamah, "I always entered the Aqsa Mosque . . . which was occupied by the Knights Templars, who were my friends. The Templars would evacuate the little adjoining mosque so that I might pray in it."

Zwi Werblowski sums up the Muslim position: "It is true

that for Islam, Jerusalem is not a holy city in the Jewish sense of that expression. . . . But the very fact that the noble *haram* —'the surrounding of which we have blessed'—is there, creates an almost natural presumption that it should be part of the *dar al Islam* ['under Muslim sovereignty']."

Basically, what Israeli liberals wanted was to neutralize Arab national and religious aspirations and divert their energies into nonpolitical channels. Israeli liberals could do nothing to remove Arab feelings of injustice and frustration, for the causes of these feelings were Israeli national policies with which they themselves identified. The only path open to them was to deal with the problems of a neutral character in the hope that coping with them successfully would, in some miraculous manner, dissipate the underlying conflict.

The "neutral" areas were at first extensive, because the Israeli establishment and public opinion ignored the Arabs, viewing them as a manipulable object. During the initial period, liberal officials could operate with relative freedom. Matters traditionally considered indispensable for the system of control of the Israeli Arabs, such as intervention in religious matters, school curriculum, and Arab economic and social institutions—were handled differently in Jerusalem: the Palestinians were left alone to manage their own affairs.

The "neutral" areas shrank gradually, however, as positions stiffened and Arab resistance became more vocal. The heroic years of innovative policies ended with the demise of Moshe Dayan after the 1973 war. The painful awakening caused by the Yom Kippur War and the ascendancy of the Palestine Liberation Organization—the realization that economic development and extension of benefits of the Israeli welfare state had not only *not* diminished the level of tension but had rather exacerbated it—brought back the traditional approach. The basic Israeli perception of being the only legitimate collective in the land, and therefore viewing all Palestinian communal objectives as illegitimate, served again as the guideline for dealing with the Arab population. The traditional approach—exclusionary, adversarial, seeing any independent Arab organization as subversive and therefore as having to be eliminated—was restored.

The opaque glass wall that divided Jewish and Arab neighborhoods in Jerusalem under the Mandate was replaced for nineteen years by the barbed-wire armistice line. Its removal was done with such zeal, it can only be described as an act of faith. All signs of physical partition—sniper walls, barbed wire, military positions—were removed without trace. Roads, sewerage, water, and telephone grids severed since 1948 were reconnected. As usual, a biblical verse was found to sanction the endeavor: "Jerusalem is builded as a city that is compact [in Hebrew, *hubra*—"connected"] together" (Psalms 122:3). It was a great symbolic act signifying the return to our holy places, to the marketplace, to the Jewish Quarter in the Old City. But in all truth it also represented a deeply sincere hope for reconciliation with the Arabs. The removal of physical barriers was perceived as a sign of the removal of mental barriers. It was hoped that a new era of peaceful coexistence would dawn upon us, and bridges would be constructed over the sectarian divide. What really came to pass was a gradual restoration of the wall, but now it resembled not a glass wall but a one-way mirror with gates that could be opened from one side only. Only the Israelis could watch the Arabs and enter their territory at will, while for the Arabs the wall was inpenetrable and the gates closed.

Some years ago I participated in a "dialogue" with West Bank Palestinians held in, of all places, West Berlin. The organizers, wanting to give us a respite from our painful discussions, had arranged a visit to East Berlin. A Palestinian friend who had crossed over in the past told me that he would not join us. "Why?" I asked. "Aren't you interested?" "Very much," he replied. "But I have my own reasons, which I'll explain only after you return safely."

An uneasy feeling of vulnerability overcomes you when you leave Checkpoint Charlie and cross no-man's-land. You open an iron gate to enter the East German checkpoint and realize that it opens only from the outside. Once you are in, you cannot go back. The soldier in the booth looks up, but not at your face. You realize that there is a mirror hidden from you above his head. He inspects your passport, and the short inspection seems to you endless. He nods, and then you pass through three more gates—all opened from the outside only —and finally find yourself in the land of the socialist dream. The way out is even more intimidating: the gates electronically controlled, the inspection more thorough, your passport taken, then returned; a buzz opens the last gate and you are back at Checkpoint Charlie, relieved beyond words. Paranoid? Possibly. Yet what was it that really bothered me? It was the loss of control, the feeling that you are at the mercy of alien forces whose actions and motivations are totally strange, who may decide to deprive you of your liberty because you have violated laws unknown to you. It is the arbitrariness that bothers you. When we returned to our hotel, my Palestinian friend asked how it was. I described my feelings. "Now I'll tell you why I did not come. What you have experienced is what I feel when I return home from overseas: the same feeling of total helplessness when your security officer singles me out for a thorough inspection at Ben-Gurion Airport. I have to go through it because I want to return home. I don't need that aggravation for mere sightseeing."

Jerusalem is not Berlin. There is no concrete wall and no checkpoints except occasionally following terrorist acts; there is free movement of people, the city functions as one physical entity, and even the presence of security forces is less visible than, say, policemen in New York. Yet for one third of the population the system seems arbitrary and their control over their own destiny seems very limited. The Palestinians are totally at the mercy of a regime whose national policies are diametrically opposed to their own aspirations. They repudiate its basic legitimacy and therefore are considered potential enemies. Their houses can be searched at any moment, their youth detained, their land expropriated, and their freedom of movement limited. Their basic insecurity about their personal and communal future forces them to retreat to the shelter of their houses and neighborhoods, where they huddle together in the company of their own kind. The threat of the unknown and the growing despair motivates them back to the fold of religion, to the security of Islamic fundamentalism. They acquire even the exterior behavior of an insecure minority. Two Palestinian scholars came to visit me in my office in West Jerusalem not long ago. It was late afternoon, and being immersed in the discussion, I had not noticed the falling dusk. A Jewish colleague who had recently arrived from Europe remarked on the lateness of the hour. The Palestinians, visibly relieved, took their leave. My Jewish friend apologized for the interruption: "I had noticed their uneasiness and realized what was going on in their minds: they were worried about returning home from the Jewish sector at night—that they will be stopped at a roadblock. You don't understand this, but their look was just like mine when I find myself in an alien environment full of goyim."

In the industrial area of Jerusalem you find many Arab workers who have assumed Hebrew names. Some even wear yarmulkes. Almost all Arabs are fluent in colloquial Hebrew, while very few Israelis have bothered to acquire even basic Arabic. You always find Jewish customers in Arab stores and workshops, but very few Arabs stroll in the Jewish sector except for work. Arabs have also acquired the positive aspects of a threatened minority. They have attained self-sufficiency in almost all personal and communal matters, keeping their contacts with and reliance on the Israeli system to a minimum. They have created and maintained their own elaborate networks in the economic, judicial, and social spheres, all totally independent and voluntary.

Perhaps the most powerful reaction to the new condition of a helpless minority is the tremendous quest for learning, especially the development of higher education. The Palestinians have always pursued higher education and are known to have the highest per capita ratio of university graduates in the Arab world. But the development of institutions of learning, research facilities, publication of newspapers, magazines, and books under occupation is truly phenomenal. Visitors who come to Jerusalem after touring the Arab countries are surprised to see the vitality of Palestinian youth living under occupation, compared to the relative apathy of their peers in Amman or Damascus. The challenge of occupation, the exigencies of living under an alien regime, the basic need not to allow oneself to succumb to impotence—all these contribute to the seeming paradox of a helpless yet vibrant and vital Palestinian minority.

It is ironic that although the Palestinians have assumed the traditional Jewish role of a threatened minority, the Israelis are unable to shed that self-image. Although they outnumber the Palestinians in Jerusalem at a ratio of two to one and have a firm hold on all positions of power, Israelis still view themselves as a threatened minority. Arab terrorist acts are perceived in the context of anti-Semitic pogroms. We are obsessed with security; the perception of every hostile act as a threat to the very existence of the state underlies the Israeli sense of insecurity. Our self-image is a curious mixture of arrogant confidence and profound vulnerability.

Studies of Northern Ireland suggest that the intensity of the conflict between Catholics and Protestants can be partially explained by what is termed the "double minority syndrome." Both Catholics and Protestants feel and act as a besieged minority. They display insecurity and stress characteristic of a threatened minority, and hold inflexible political positions typical of insecure groups. The reason for that syndrome is that Protestants are indeed a majority in Ulster but a minority on the whole island of Ireland, and the Catholics are just the opposite. The same syndrome can be identified in Jerusalem. The Israelis are indeed a majority in Jerusalem and in Palestine as a whole, but they are a tiny minority in the Middle East. The Arabs are just the opposite. The result is that both feel threatened and act as if they are a besieged minority. One cannot deny the feeling of insecurity and stress of the Palestinians, but one can equally not dismiss the same feeling among the Jews as mere paranoia. The stress is especially strong among the Jews, because for them the minority syndrome is second nature. It was their status for thousands of years, and memories of persecution, especially of the Holocaust, are connected to being a defenseless minority. A group representing Jews who settled in the new neighborhoods came to the municipality during the Yom Kippur War. They demanded protection. "We are encircled by the Arabs," they claimed. At that time their number was double the size of the adjacent Arab population. The "double minority syndrome" explains the intensity of the conflict and the need of both communities to display inflexible and exclusionary positions. The minority role-orientation explains the Jewish-Arab dichotomy. All minorities perceive themselves as living in a world divided in two: our side and the other side. They interpret events in dichotomous terms; dichotomous perceptions permeate every interaction, define interests, and establish rigid borderlines. Everything is seen in terms of the groups' gain or loss. They have no interest in history for its own sake. It is, however, part of the perpetual battle cry, an ally of sorts that provides ammunition for fighting the "other side," for strengthening the unity of the group, or for seeking "justice." Settling scores and rectifying wrongs of the past are perceived as possessing higher moral values than universal norms of justice.

An Arab resident of the Jewish Quarter in the Old City, whose house was expropriated, applied to the government agency in charge of restoring the area for permission to buy back his house rather than be evicted. When his application was denied, he petitioned the High Court of Justice. A Supreme Court judge, known for his concern for human rights, rejected the petition on various grounds, including the following: ". . . Third, the need for reconstructing the Jewish Quarter in the Old City emerged only because the armies of Jordan invaded it, expelled the Jews, looted their property, and demolished their houses. In the nature of things the reconstruction came to restore the glory of the Jewish settlement in the Old City as of old, so that the Jews will once again have a quarter for themselves. . . . Fourth, if there is discrimination against Jordanian citizens owing allegiance to the Kingdom of Jordan, this discrimination seems justified and proper to me. We lament and deplore the evils that the Jordanians committed against us in the Old City, and it cannot be demanded of us that we shall open the gates wide to them to return and settle precisely in the Jewish Quarter. One can explain and justify such discrimination in terms of security and political considerations." It doesn't matter that the Jewish Quarter was captured and destroyed during a full-fledged war (1948), in the course of which scores of Arab quarters were conquered and taken over. It is of no consequence that the petitioner was forced to become a Jordanian subject after 1948 and now finds himself as an alien resident in Israel, that he seeks to keep his ancestral home, that he challenges the morality of allocating houses according to ethnic affiliations. He must personally pay for the evils that "they" committed to "us." One cannot escape one's basic role as Arab or Jew, just as one cannot escape the basic role of sex or age. Universal values do not apply beyond the sectarian divide, and double standards can always be explained by security and political considerations. Everything is a matter of survival, just like at war. The inevitable consequences of war psychology are the dehumanization of the enemy, the attribution of demonic qualities to his behavior, the blurring of the enemy's individual, human features and instead the creation of a faceless mass of menacing crowds. The enemy acquires a generic name: Boche, Limey, Cossack, Zionist, or Ahmad. The mere recognition of the "other side" as human, capable of expressing normal sensitivities, amounts to heresy.

Israeli soldiers and relatives of soldiers fallen during the 1967 war improvised, after the end of the hostilities, memorials in various parts of East Jerusalem where military actions took place. One year later the government replaced the memorials with permanent, uniform marble plaques. The Arabs, whether prompted to commemorate their own dead or adopting the idea from the Jews, reacted by erecting their own temporary memorials. At first we did not react to the erection of Arab memorials, but when we saw their number increase daily, we decided to act. I was sent to negotiate with the Arab leadership and reach an agreement. We had agreed that the temporary memorials be dismantled and four permanent plaques erected at specific locations. Plans were submitted and approved, and the Arabs began to erect a memorial on a conspicuous site near the city wall. Until that moment the matter had been kept secret, but then the Arabs decided to release the story to a Jewish journalist. When I was approached for comment, I confirmed the story and added: "Seventy thousand Arab inhabitants wished to erect monuments in memory of their dead, and there is no reason in the world why it should not be allowed. When people die, no political accounts remain, and the memory of the dead should be honored. I hope Jewish public opinion will show understanding."

This was a naïve hope. The Jewish public was shocked, and the matter was brought up in the Knesset and subsequently in the cabinet. A public opinion poll showed that 67 percent of the Jewish population opposed the erection of Arab monuments; 18 percent felt that "losers have no rights"; 28 percent contended that "those who intended to exterminate us should not be commemorated." A sample of press reaction includes the following comments: "Is this the hour to put up monuments to the glory and splendor of the murderers of our people; to those who received orders by their king to 'kill Jews wherever they found them'? What if neo-Nazis get up tomorrow and decide to erect a monument to Adolf Eichmann in Jerusalem? He too was a soldier. It would be hard to conceive even today, 30 years after the blitz raids on Britain, that it would enter the heads of the relatives of Luftwaffe pilots to demand the erection of memorials in Trafalgar Square!" There were, of course, other voices who claimed that the Arabs "are destined to accept a regime they did not choose—to feel they are both losers and a minority—as they have been so destined, it is our duty to defuse the justified bitterness even if it was not we who caused it." Despite the furor, we stood firm and allowed the completion of the memorial. I paid dearly for my share in that controversy; since then, I was permanently stigmatized as an "Arab lover," and my subsequent actions were carefully compiled in a formidable dossier, which at the appropriate moment led to my demotion.

The controversy over the memorials prompted me to study how other people commemorate their fallen soldiers, and how dead enemies are treated. I went to the obvious place—to Verdun. Here almost half a million French, German, and Americans found their death and 800,000 were wounded or gassed during the First World War. The signs of the worst carnage in the annals of warfare are almost obliterated. Thick shrubbery and dense fir forests shroud the shell holes, the trenches, and the bunkers. The huge, subterranean forts are commercialized, each with its souvenir shop. But the cemeteries, the cemeteries: more than one hundred thousand crosses, white in the French and American cemeteries, black in the German, and among them, a pathetic handful of Stars of David, the resting place of my Jewish brothers who fell fighting one another in the service of their respective countries; and the Douaumont Ossuary—the huge forbidding structure where 150,000 unknown soldiers are buried, their remains collected for decades from the battlefields.

The French memorials are evocative, patriotic: the fallen lion marking the closest point to Verdun reached by the Germans; the "skeleton memorial" on the summit of Mort Homme. The inscriptions are heroic: the famous battle cry "Ils ne passeront pas," coined in Verdun and resonated since in many a battlefield from Madrid to Stalingrad. But there is also a small plaque at Fort Vaux: "To my son, since your eyes were closed, mine have never ceased to cry"; and there are the Hebrew letters of the Ten Commandments on the memorial for the Jewish soldiers—"Frenchmen, aliens and volunteers" —overlooking a sea of crosses. The German cemeteries are located near the French, in some places close to memorials for French hostages and deportees shot by the Nazis during the

Second World War. They are well cared for, although deserted; rows of black iron crosses interspersed by slate headstones with Stars of David and Hebrew inscriptions. There are no patriotic inscriptions; a simple slab at the entrance bears the factual sentence in German and French: "Here repose German soldiers." How civilized it is, I reflected, that despite the animosity, the memories of two world wars, and the atrocities of the Nazis, these fallen enemies' eternal rest is not disturbed. How absurd it is that one can feel compassion only for a dead enemy, and even that is unfortunately not the case in Jerusalem.

Years later, while watching a war movie, I understood why. I saw the hero searching the pockets of a dead enemy for documents. He opens the dead man's wallet, and snapshots of a smiling wife and innocent children fall out. This is the transition point from the savage, belligerent environment, where for killing one receives a citation, to normal, peacetime conditions, when one is hanged for it. In my naïveté I thought that the war in Jerusalem was over and it was time to resume humanistic values. I had not realized that warlike perceptions are endemic to the polarized environment and that by demanding Jewish understanding of Arab sensitivities, I confused them. As long as they perceive their conflict as a war of survival, they cannot view their enemy as human. Your finger trembles on the trigger when you think about the target as a breathing, caring father.

All this seems farfetched, extreme, and esoteric to many Israelis, who vehemently refute my description of the Jerusalem environment. For many Israelis the conflict in Jerusalem is a relatively mild and quite normal tension caused by cultural, pluralistic, and religious frictions. After all, the city is calm; there are fewer violent deaths in Jerusalem than, say, in Cleveland, Ohio. People do not interact through gunsights, as at war; they live normal lives, although admittedly there is latent tension and occasional violence. Indeed, to depict Jerusalem as a polarized community seems to most Israelis an exaggeration; it is more convenient to term it "multicultural" or "heterogeneous." Mayor Teddy Kollek is the great exponent of Jerusalem as a "mosaic of cultures, never a melting pot." Each year he organizes a "conference of heterogeneous cities." Mayors of other heterogeneous cities such as Boston and Chicago join him to discuss mutual problems of planning and decentralization of city government to allow "people of various neighborhoods to feel some increasing control over their own lives and the decision-making process."

There are no trench lines dividing the Jewish and the Arab communities, not even a "peace line" separating them as there is between adversarial communities in Belfast or Nicosia. The communities interact in the streets, in factories, and through the common sewerage system. At war both real and perceived environments are dichotomized. In Jerusalem, the real environment is a fairly integrated urban system. It is the perceived reality that makes Jerusalem a polarized city, the arena of an intense conflict. One doesn't have to be a soldier manning the trenches to feel at war. If the issues at stake are thought to be of the greatest importance, if they involve one's most cherished cultural, national, and material values and rewards, if one considers them inalienable rights and is ready to struggle for them, then he perceives himself at war even while pursuing his civilian life. In communal conflicts such as the Jerusalem conflict, both communities define the issues at stake in such terms. Just as in shooting wars, the majority are armchair soldiers, but there is no doubt about the intensity of the communal sentiment. There are fewer casualties in perceived wars, but in the long run communal conflicts are more devastating than shooting wars. The latter are waged until one side is victorious or until both sides are exhausted. Then everybody can go home. Communal conflicts are endemic and have no ultimate solution; they just drag on and on.

Israeli liberals, like all liberals, abhor dichotomies. Their harmonious world view prevents them from perceiving the conflict in such terms. After all, why should they paint a gloomy picture? They have attained their own national objectives. Now they have only to defend the political status quo against external forces and against their own troubled conscience. They express their unease by defining the problem in universal, civil-libertarian terms. The conflict is the struggle of an underprivileged minority for a larger share of the common cake. The conflict is caused by discrimination in housing, in economic and educational opportunities, and by lack of equality in civil rights. Arab grievances are apolitical; politics is the cause of the conflict rather than its outcome.

The struggle for civil rights and equality is very appealing. It is also safe, because it does not clash with the Israeli national consensus. It also shows how a "manageable" solution can be reached by a convenient perception of the problem. One defines for the minority its grievances, and works to bring about remedies. But, alas, the minority itself never defines itself as second-class citizens. The Arabs reject the comparison of their status to that of Puerto Ricans or blacks in the U.S. because the comparison implies that their present situation is permanent and they are absorbed into the Israeli society. They consider themselves under occupation, which is by definition a temporary situation bound to be terminated one day. Arabs are not struggling for a better position within the Israeli system but rather for the liberation from their forced integration into it. All their inequalities are subsumed in their basic political inequality, which they refuse to correct within the framework of the Israeli system. Criteria for evaluating inequalities are set in the context of an accepted and legitimized political framework. If one repudiates the system, one does not seek redress within it. The Arabs seek self-government rather than good government; they are not interested in a larger slice of the pie—they want to bake their own. The existing inequalities are therefore accepted as an inevitable consequence of their status as an occupied people.

Israeli civil libertarians cannot participate in that struggle; they are unable to identify with the basic political grievance of the Arabs because it contradicts their own cherished national posture. They cannot admit to themselves that the basic inequality lies in their imposed regime, that their system is based on their coercion. Therefore, they explain it differently. Teddy Kollek sees Arab resistance as caused by intimidation. He wrote, "To discuss the future of Jerusalem with local Arab leaders is more complex because of PLO threats against even the most patriotic Arab moderates who would dare in any way to lend semblance of legitimacy to Israeli rule." Yet in another place he must admit, "I am certain that the moment the Arabs of Jerusalem believed they could get rid of us, they would do so." It is heartbreaking for a liberal to admit that the city is held together by force and that if Israeli coercive power were taken away, the city would split on its ethnic fault line.

We all try to cope with our incongruities. Our actions, positions, and decisions are bound to be eclectic. Painful dilemmas force unpleasant compromises; the temptation to leave the arena, to abandon the role of a participant is strong. Yet only participants can influence the course of events. One remains within the system only to become increasingly tangled in one's own compromises. One seldom has the courage or the time to realize how far one had drifted. One day, many years ago, I was invited with a colleague of mine, one of Dayan's advisers on the West Bank, to lunch with a South African official on a visit to Jerusalem. During lunch we discussed our work, and the visitor showed great interest in our ideas on how to improve Israeli-Palestinian relations by leaving the Palestinians alone to manage their own affairs. Suddenly he said, "How would you react if we were to invite you to advise the new regime in Transkei?" We were shocked. His query implied that he considered our work comparable with their reactionary, racist schemes in the Bantustans. When we expressed our indignation, he smiled and said, "I understand your reaction. But aren't we actually doing the same thing? We are faced with the same existential problem, therefore we arrive at the same solution. The only difference is that yours is pragmatic and ours is ideological. Yes, we are all in love with our own compromises." Naturally we rejected the offer. I did not accept the comparison then, and I do not today. But I learned an important lesson: it is all a matter of context. The same concepts may be moral, liberal, and progressive but may also be immoral, reactionary, and repressive depending on one's intentions and the political and social circumstances under which one operates. "Separation" can mean a liberal policy that recognizes plurality and seeks through equal treatment to preserve the unique identity of diverse ethnic groups. It can be a euphemism for discrimination, a reactionary and prejudiced policy aimed at repressing the minority and dispossessing it. The concept by itself is neutral, and sometimes even the policies are identical; the difference is in the context.

Consider spatial separation, the ethnically segregated pattern of Jerusalem's neighborhoods. I have emphasized earlier the voluntary aspect of the trend of different communities to live in ethnically homogeneous neighborhoods. Teddy Kollek is one of the chief advocates of segregation. He wrote, "We don't have integrated Arab-Jewish neighborhoods. But there is no segregation between Jews and Arabs in the law. There is nothing to prevent an Arab from buying or renting an apartment in an otherwise Jewish building or vice versa. It just does not work like that. If an Arab has children, he will want to send them to an Arab neighborhood school, and he and his wife will want to be near their friends, their mosque, the markets, the very smells and sounds they know. The same is true not only for Jews, but for Armenians and all other sects and ethnic groups as well."

Development of ethnically homogeneous neighborhoods is the official urban-planning policy of Jerusalem. It is formulated in official planning directives thus: "Preservation of the unity of Jerusalem by siting neighborhoods in a form that would create a nonpolarized mosaic of communities." This policy can be interpreted as a benign, coexistence-oriented attempt to allow for separate, uninterrupted ethnic and cultural development of diverse groups. It satisfies the basic need of Jews and Arabs to cluster around their own kind, and it decreases the level of intercommunal tension caused by living in close proximity to people with different cultural lifestyles. Yet this is only one side of the coin. The same policy serves also as a mask to hide discriminatory policies toward the Arabs in resource allocation for infrastructure, housing, and welfare services. The gap between the Jewish and the Arab neighborhoods is enormous. Ninety percent of public resources were invested in the Jewish neighborhoods, and only 10 percent in the Arab sector. The vast discrepancy between the modern, well-planned, illuminated, green Jewish neighborhoods and the old, rundown Arab quarters is glaring. The authorities do not see any contradiction between separate development, peaceful coexistence policies, and the aggressive penetration of Arab areas for building vast new Jewish neighborhoods. Construction of new, exclusively Jewish housing developments on land confiscated from Arabs is viewed, indeed, as an expansion of the benign "mosaic" principle: "Everyone belongs to one community or another, with its separate language and traditions; that is part of Jerusalem's traditional character, and all the new housing will undoubtedly not change it," concludes Teddy Kollek. Yet to understand Kollek's predicament, his compromises, and the true meaning of "separation," one should juxtapose that statement with another from the same book, *For Jerusalem:* "The Arabs of East Jerusalem would like their part of the city to revert to Arab sovereignty, and this cannot come about if the area is geographically cut off from Arab territory by new Jewish suburbs."

In the context of Jerusalem, where the whole Jewish-Arab conflict is encapsulated, where there exists a basic political inequality between the two sides, separate and equal is a contradiction in terms. If liberals themselves accept political inequality as justified and proper, then separation must assume a reactionary significance, implemented only when it does not interfere with ethnocentrist imperatives.

Separation under the British Mandate was voluntary, not

imposed by one side. Basic political inequality did not exist, for Jews and Arabs were equally ranked, both lacking direct access to state coercive machinery. Under those circumstances, separate and equal were not contradictory, as Edward Said claims. However, Teddy Kollek's claim that post-1967 separation is liberal and benign is equally wrong. Now Jews and Arabs are not equally ranked, and the Jews use their monopoly over state coercive power to advance their partisan interests, also through imposed separation. Separation is indeed "Jerusalem's traditional character," but its meaning is a matter of context.

During my tenure as administrator of East Jerusalem I was involved in several working groups whose task it was to draft proposals for comprehensive political solutions for Jerusalem as well as for specific disputes in the city. I also assembled a staff to study previous peace plans. We listed no less than thirty-one major proposals put forward since 1916, when Jerusalem emerged as an international problem. I thought how sad it was that so much creative energy had been invested, and it all came to naught. I realized that the reason was not lack of impartiality, expertise, or creativity on the part of the authors but rather the inability of the sides directly involved to accept a compromise. Their perception of the game as one in which only one side can win prevented them from exploring the possibility that both sides may gain from the compromise. Those who tried to play the frustrating game of devising political solutions for Jerusalem believed that there are no real zero-sum games, only those perceived as such. They perceived themselves as being "above" or "outside" the conflict, and therefore qualified to view it objectively and to be accepted as an honest broker. There is an arrogant element of Solomonic judgment in their posture. Unable to realize that in a polarized environment there can be no "involved objective outsider," they attempted to invent a sensible impartial and just solution—in the middle. But the sides were too far apart and rigidly entrenched. The real problem did not lie in the lack of theoretical compromises but rather in the lack of willingness to consider a compromise—not unilateral willingness, but mutual and simultaneous.

The study of the magnificent exercise in futility did not hinder me from putting my own hand in the fire—with the inevitable consequences. Between 1968 and 1977 there were regular contacts between King Hussein and Israeli ministers, as well as between high-ranking Israeli and Jordanian officials. These contacts have shown, as expected, that the Jerusalem problem is a major stumbling block to an agreement between the two countries. In the summer of 1968 a group of officials from the Foreign Ministry, the Defense Ministry, and myself were asked to suggest a plan whose objective according to the terms of reference was "to ensure the unity of Jerusalem under our sovereignty, and at the same time to satisfy non-Israeli (especially Jordanian) interest." In short, how to square the circle. After giving the problem some thought, in July 1968 I submitted a proposal that later gained some notoriety under the name "the Borough Plan." I suggested the creation of "a single municipal county under dual sovereignty." The proposal called for the creation of a new municipal district—"Greater Jerusalem"— which would include united Jerusalem and the rest of the metropolitan area that was not annexed to Israel. The administration of this county with dual sovereignty (the annexed and nonannexed areas) would be similar to that of the Greater London Council, that is, there would be a division into boroughs with an overall, federal or "roof" municipality. Each borough would be ethnically homogeneous and would have defined powers and responsibilities. Both Israeli and Jordanian governments would have a say in the activities of the roof municipality by virtue of their sovereignty over part of the territory of Greater Jerusalem. It was an attempt at making the cake bigger and dividing it anew, or a device to "blur" the sovereignty issue by delegating national government functions to local government, traditionally considered less political and more of a street-level delivery system. My proposal, complete with maps, statistics, and a detailed plan of the powers and responsibilities of the three-tier, rather cumbersome administrative structure, was submitted to the Foreign Ministry, but nothing came of it. The contacts with the Jordanians never developed into a meaningful dialogue; the distance between the two sides was too great for them to reach a common denominator. There was another reason. Some proposals submitted to the Jordanians were leaked to the Israeli public, and they created an outcry so strong that the politicians were forced to deny their existence. In April 1971 my turn came. The "Borough Plan" was leaked to the press in order to sabotage my political career. It turned into something of a cause célèbre under the name "the Benvenisti affair." A campaign of vilification—which included threats of murder—was organized against me by a right-wing group called DOV (the Hebrew word for bear became the acronym for "repression of traitors"). Slogans were daubed on city walls calling me a traitor. One of them said: "Let's divide Benvenisti—not Jerusalem." Bodyguards followed me and my pregnant wife, and drivers spat in my face at traffic lights. The campaign was not limited to fringe groups. In a Knesset debate, called as a result of the scandal, several members of the Knesset quoted extensively from a dossier that somebody compiled, listing all my "pro-Arab" activities. They included, of course, my agreement to erect Arab war memorials, and also others: my refusal to allow a Jewish takeover of shops in the main bazaar in the Old City, a futile struggle against illegal excavation under Muslim religious seminaries along the northern part of the Western Wall, and the transformation of the excavated vaults into Orthodox synagogues; warnings concerning schemes to open underground passages leading to the Temple Mount; and permission to clean, restore, and reuse a fifteenth-century Mameluke bazaar requested by the Supreme Muslim Council. An honorable member of the Knesset later to become minister of justice demanded that I be brought to trial for treason. The foreign minister, Abba Eban, under attack not only from the opposition but also from members of his own Labor party, denied that he had even heard of the proposal before it was leaked, and he stated that it had never been adopted by his ministry. The government had escaped a vote of censure only by an assurance to the National Religious party that repair work on the railways would be stopped on the Sabbath in exchange for their support. I became such a political liability that even Mayor Kollek was forced to abandon me until the storm passed.

The Arabs found the whole affair comic. One of them wrote me, "I thought you were more knowledgeable. Do you really think that your Zionist scheme to retain East Jerusalem under your sovereignty could serve as a genuine basis for negotiations?" My ill-fated proposal was not the only one put forward. There were even more esoteric schemes. One called for the "Vaticanization" of the Temple Mount. It was suggested that the mosques be given extraterritorial status and be administrated by Jordan, "which would represent the Muslim world." A special guard—a Muslim "Swiss Guard"—was to be placed on the Mount in order to ensure Muslims from the Arab countries free access, and so that the "Saudi king would not have to step on Israeli soil and receive an Israeli visa on his way to al-Aqsa Mosque." It was suggested that a special access road be constructed and placed under Muslim sovereignty. Later it was suggested that instead of a road, a tunnel be dug. Another scheme called for the creation of three religious boroughs in the Old City. All these proposals were never discussed and were never leaked. Their authors had no political enemies.

I learned the hard way what I had already suspected: that "resolvers" are frustrated peacemakers who believe that communal conflicts are like a chessboard where one can think up the best arrangement of chess pieces and move them all at once. What they fail to understand is that there is an inherent contradiction in their logic. Their attempt is a third-party intervention into a binary situation. Therefore, it is at best irrelevant and at worst becomes part of the dichotomy—

rejected by both sides or identified by one side as aligned with the other.

I became extremely wary of the discipline called "conflict resolution," especially of the branch specializing in producing manuals for resolving conflicts in easy steps. One winter not long ago I participated in a workshop for resolving the Israeli-Palestinian conflict held at a distinguished American university. Our workshop was squeezed between similar workshops dealing with the "Northern Ireland conflict" and the "Cyprus conflict." My frustration grew slowly until at a formal dinner I had one glass too many. I stood up and said to the organizer, a "resolver" par excellence, "I wonder if you know who we are at all. For all you care, we can be Zimbabweans, Basques, Arabs, Jews, Catholics, Protestants, Greeks, Turks. To you we are just guinea pigs to be tested, or at best to be engineered." To his credit, I hasten to add, he stood up and, with tears in his eyes, said, "Thank you, I needed that."

Peace proposals are useful if they are part of a process in which the parties are brought to the point where they can agree on a specific settlement. This is a long process that should involve concrete steps to break down distrust and build up the possibility that peace could be perceived as mutually beneficial. In themselves, peace proposals are constructive, meaningless, or counterproductive depending, again, on the context.

After I left city government in 1978, I heard that Mayor Kollek had revived the "Borough Plan." He wrote, "I had envisioned a future structure in Jerusalem under which the city would be governed through a network of boroughs. Each borough would have a great deal of autonomy over its municipal services and its life-style." He assigned a distinguished Israeli jurist to prepare a draft constitution for the borough structure and began to build a network of "neighborhood administrations" in various sectors of the city, both Jewish and Arab. The scheme was presented to foreign visitors not as a plan for the decentralization of Jerusalem's local government but as a major component in a plan for the solution of the Jerusalem problem on the international level. I thought that the revival of the plan was not only ridiculous but positively wrong. Although it resembled superficially my old proposal, there was a fundamental difference. Mine was drawn within the specific context of ongoing (although sporadic) peace negotiations. It contained one indispensable element: the satisfaction of Arab claims for sovereignty. Without recognition of political equality, a low-level municipal autonomy is meaningless. The revised Borough Plan was based on the convenient premise that the conflict in Jerusalem is over the control of sewerage and street-lighting, a variation on the apolitical "mosaic" theme.

Two American jurists invited me to get together and discuss the new Borough Plan. They too were asked to study it. After I explained my reservations, one of them asked why I was so antagonistic: "If it won't do any good, at least it won't do any harm." "Ah," I said, "and what about the legitimacy that you give the existing setup? Would you accept an invitation to advise on the constitution of Transkei? Your work on the boroughs implies an acceptance of a basic political inequality between Jews and Arabs. Jews will have a monopoly over all political power, and Arabs will be allowed 'a great deal of autonomy over their municipal services'! The present system is bad enough. Don't give it a semblance of respectability."

"Who told you that we accept the basic political inequality?" replied one jurist. "For us it is a constraint that cannot be changed at present, so we try to operate within parameters of existing political conditions." It was a valid argument. We represented two legitimate approaches: One was solution-oriented, which measures actions by approximation of their possible results to a desired goal. The other position is process-oriented, which measures actions by success in coping with an endemic situation. Returning to what I said before, you could call one approach principled, resembling kibbutz social ideology, and the other pragmatic, on the lines of the Boy Scout ethos. One approach abhors the status quo and is fearful that coping with its symptoms would perpetuate an unacceptable situation; the other seeks to help people live with the problem, hoping that time and changing circumstances and attitudes will eventually create an environment susceptible to solution. The former position is a consistent ideological framework; the latter reconciles ideological imperatives with the exigencies of daily life.

The communal conflict in Jerusalem is endemic because it is a bewildering mixture of national-level sovereignty issues with local-level disputes over allocation of resources and local political control. Even in the unlikely event that a political solution is found, Jews and Arabs will always quarrel over budgets and on the position of fire chief. Alternative political structures can be debated endlessly at high-level ministerial and diplomatic conferences. The local leadership finds itself constantly dealing with housing, taxation, and education. They must cope with the symptoms, and reconcile their partisan, nationalist positions with their roles as providers of life-supporting functions to the entire community, and their responsibility to keep the conflict at a bearable level. Under such circumstances the pragmatic, symptomatic approach is undoubtedly more appropriate. The consistent, solution-oriented approach is admirable but ultimately useless. It provides profound analyses and scathing criticism but no constructive suggestions on how to deal with the actual problems.

I began my involvement as a pragmatic, process-oriented practitioner. I believed that my duty was to alleviate hardship, to minimize tension, and to foster coexistence. I had no set political goals except coping with the immediate symptoms of the conflict, which were serious enough. My Israeli-Zionist ideology, my professional training, and my liberal world view clashed all too often, but I was not confused by the contradictions. I was merely a troubleshooter. I did not hesitate to be party to a decision to demolish the house of a terrorist before his trial—and to issue a building license for the same house a few months later; I tried to limit the size of land expropriation but set up an office to compensate Arabs for confiscated land. I participated in overseeing the works at the Western Wall area but cooperated with the Muslim authorities to safeguard their property there. I fought a decision to retaliate to a grenade attack by evicting innocent civilian Arab families from their houses but volunteered to carry out the eviction peacefully and humanely. I approved a request to build an Arab war memorial but ordered the removal of other memorials built illegally. I tried to reinstate the Arab municipality, dispersed after the annexation, but organized massive Arab participation in the first Israeli municipal election after the annexation. All these actions were inconsistent as far as a desired goal is concerned, whether partisan, professional, or ideological. There was only a consistent effort to deal with the symptom of a malaise that already seemed endemic.

But in a city where electricity is "Jewish" and "Arab," and two ethnic blood banks exist, there is no place for an administrator whose job is to deal impartially with community relations. My actions were scrutinized on two levels: Israeli partisan actions seemed appropriate, normal, and obvious—therefore ignored; actions aimed at helping Arabs seemed harmful and unpatriotic—therefore deplored. As most Israeli officials stayed away from the Arab population, I found myself dealing almost exclusively with Arab problems. No wonder all my actions were perceived as ideologically "pro-Arab."

The ideological role was forced upon me, and given my temperament, I took up the challenge and made my position clear. It was only a matter of time before I had to leave. Other people stayed within the system and tried to pursue the symptomatic approach. I admire them, but what worries me is that with the institutionalization of the dual, unequal system in Jerusalem, their role had willy-nilly become ideological. The mere fact that they stay in office legitimizes the system. People say that if they are still there, it cannot be that bad.

As the years turn into decades I wonder how much I myself had contributed to the legitimization of the system. It may well be that the genuine, humane attempts to lessen communal tension and alleviate hardship had facilitated the "partisans" in imposing their ethnocentristic goals with minimum opposition and optimal public relations. But what else could I have done?

Be that as it may, both Muhammad and myself are good examples of what the Reverend Dr. Ian Paisley has to say about people like us: "A traitor and a bridge are very much alike; both go over to the other side." He was referring to another polarized community—the Northern Irish—but I can think of a number of Israelis who would endorse his aphorism. It would be unfair, however, to lump Muhammad and myself together—unfair to Muhammad. Inequality persists even in punishment. He was thrown into jail; I remained free to reflect, study, and even to participate in political life. After all, I still belong to the dominating group. There is an old Jewish saying: "Israel, even if he has sinned, remains Israel."

I was free to search for situations comparable to the Jerusalem predicament. The feeling that your problem is not unique gives you some comfort. It was not difficult to find many polarized communities. In fact most major cities can be ranged on a scale of polarization. There are those that show only mild and "normal" ethnic or racial segmentation; most American cities belong in that category. There are those that show strong biethnic strife, such as Brussels and Montréal. There are cities in which the binational conflict is waged in an urban setting; Belfast and Jerusalem are examples of this unfortunate group. Finally there are those cities in which polarization resulted in complete physical partition: Nicosia, Beirut, and Berlin.

From all these cases, I found that perhaps the most comparable environments are those of Jerusalem and Belfast. One cannot imagine two more divergent physical environments than these two cities. Belfast, the shabby Victorian city lying at the foot of emerald hills on the shores of a gray lough under overcast skies; Jerusalem, the ancient city of kings and saints, perched on a ridge between the desert and the sown, basking in golden sunlight. Divergent indeed yet comparable, for I felt in Belfast that both are perceived by their citizens as a dichotomized environment. In both, the world is divided in two, while the physical environment still functions as an integrated urban system. Both are extreme cases, because the macronational dispute—exacerbated by societal, cultural, and political conditions—create a multidimensional, hopeless strife. So it was that when I visited Belfast, I had an immediate feel for the situation and could even identify with it: the constant listening to the news, the search for identifying signs in a stranger, the extreme sensitivity to controversial topics, the repeated question-plea, "When will it all end?", the division of the city into "their" part and "our" part, the separate school system, the different symbols and holidays, newspapers, sports activities, the socioeconomic inequalities.

I read a poem written by John Boyd, "Visit to School," and the following stanzas stuck in my mind:

> And schoolboys of another faith and tradition
> sit at desks, with solemn faces
> And I, expressionless, stare at each,
> conscious of the bond and break between us. . . .
> And I glance
> at each child as I call his name
> And their tired faces recall my own childhood
> in this same city, but a different childhood.

How well, I thought, he expressed my own feelings when visiting Arab schools in Jerusalem.

The more I studied Belfast, and indeed the entire "Irish question," the more I realized the similarity between Ireland and Palestine and the parallels between Belfast and Jerusalem. I also reached the gloomy conclusion that both are organic and endemic cases, and therefore intractable. I learned that there are no villains in either tale. Indeed, as the plot unfolded, the tales turned into a Greek tragedy. I was aware of the differences too. In absolute terms, the

Palestinians' deprivation in Jerusalem, defined as economic, political, social, and symbolic inequalities, is greater than Catholic deprivation in Belfast. The cultural, religious, and ideological cleavages in Jerusalem most definitely run deeper. Yet the chance that an armed ethnic confrontation similar to Belfast will develop in Jerusalem seems remote. The Israeli system of control will see to it. Richard Rose, who studied the Ulster conflict thoroughly, has observed, "Managing coercion requires skill and luck, as well as very tangible resources." The Israelis possess the skill, and are ready to commit vast material and human resources to repress Arab resistance. Arab resistance, for its part, is characterized by diffused hostility, passive attitudes, and disorganization. Yet the situation remains very volatile. As an Arab journalist has written, "Our mentality is different from the Western mentality. We react more slowly. How shall we react tomorrow to the Israeli occupation—you can never know." A friend, dealing with the threat of nuclear holocaust, had written a very plausible doomsday scenario of how a successful attempt to blow up the mosques on the Temple Mount would trigger a nuclear war involving "Muslim bombs" and "Jewish bombs."

At this point in the discourse the frustrated analyst is confronted with the inevitable query: "So, what is your suggestion? Do you have a solution?" The analyst then falls into the trap. He succumbs to the common notion that a diagnosis without a prescription is an immoral proposition and so volunteers a prescription, thus exposing himself to the same treatment he reserves for others. Thereafter the game is well known: if one does not accept the prescription, one refutes the analysis and the facts on which it is based, and all return to square one.

It is useful to ponder the definition of a "problem" in the context of a political conflict like that of Jerusalem. Usually, definition of problems dictates their perceived solution. In Jerusalem, however, it is the solution that dictates the problem and not vice versa. Convenient solutions seek cozy problems, facts to support them, and easy procedures to attain them. After all, Jerusalem is not a flat tire where one defines the problem precisely and often knows how to resolve it. For example, religious interests can be accommodated under overall exclusive sovereignty. If one wants to retain sovereignty, he can define the problem as religious, provide ample facts to substantiate his definition, and then prescribe a solution based on extraterritoriality of the holy places, which does not contradict his basic goal. I am aware that my own analysis may also be perceived as a subjective, self-serving exercise. But at least I don't suggest a prescription, and I challenge the notion that therefore the diagnosis is invalid. I concede, however, that it would be more pleasant to conclude this gloomy discourse with a constructive note, so I append some guidelines for positive thinking on Jerusalem.

Jerusalem is the key to peace between Jews and Arabs, and without a solution to the Jerusalem question there can be no durable solution to the Israeli-Palestinian conflict. All attempts to sweep the question under the rug will fail. The lump is simply too big. People of goodwill try to devise ultimate solutions. Most are brilliant and even-handed, but none could be implemented. The parties directly concerned simply refused to accept them.

The comprehensive approach is based on two premises. First, the problem is so acute, and so much depends on its solution, that it is in the interest of all parties to look for a way out and therefore a solution will be found. Second, the conflict can be resolved by devising a compromise in the middle.

It seems that both premises are not applicable to Jerusalem. The sense of urgency is not shared by all the conflicting parties. The Arabs indeed regard the problem as acute and are doing everything in their power to solve it by taking Jerusalem away from the Israelis. The Israelis, however, attach no urgency to the problem, because they are relatively content with the status quo and do not believe that a compromise can improve their situation.

The notion of a compromise is rejected prima facie by both

sides. They claim that their present positions are already painful compromises and no further concession is conceivable.

The difficulty is clearly not in devising logical and objective solutions but in coping with the perceptions of the conflicting parties. The dispute is perceived by both sides as a struggle to attain and preserve basic human needs.

Jerusalem represents for Israeli and Arab alike certain basic interests: identity, a sense of belonging to one's hometown and motherland; control over one's destiny; recognition and self-esteem; security and welfare. The political expression of these basic interests is national sovereignty, and the symbols are flags, army, capital city, and national institutions. Therefore, sovereignty and its symbols are "nonnegotiable," as one cannot give up or compromise on basic human needs.

The Israelis and the Arabs refuse to face the symmetry of their perceptions. They choose to dismiss the positions of the other side as mere propaganda, or to ignore them completely. This attitude causes many false assumptions on the nature of the conflict and in turn results in wrong conclusions.

Many believe that the conflict will vanish or will solve itself. Given the centrality of Jerusalem in the eyes of Israeli and Arab alike, this is wishful thinking. The problem will not only endure, but the cost of the continued strife will increase—for both sides. It has already cost countless lives; its continuation is bound to degenerate into ugly intercommunal violent struggle with a vicious circle of resistance-coercion-terrorism-retaliation.

The conflict is often depicted mainly as a clash of material interests that can be solved by "practical arrangements." The remainder will be left for future generations to cope with. This is an attempt to turn the conflict upside down.

While it is true that people are ready to be flexible on material interests, they insist that concessions be made under the umbrella of their own political system. First, they insist on attaining symbolic gratification in the form of sovereignty and flags. Only then can they discuss material arrangements.

The Jerusalem question is often defined as an interreligious dispute. The solution, therefore, lies in granting religious freedom and ensuring free access to and establishing extraterritorial status for the holy places. But there is no religious dispute between Jew and Muslim over any holy place, nor is there a conflict between them and Christians. The conflict is between Israeli and Arab (Muslim or Christian) over the political control of Jerusalem. Both are ready to grant the other religious freedom provided that they retain political control.

Some would like to reduce the national conflict to interethnic tension. They maintain that a system that will safeguard the cultural and communal autonomy of the minority will solve the conflict. The preservation of ethnic heritage and safeguarding of the political rights of the minority are definitely important elements. However, both sides refuse to define their political objectives as such. They consider themselves an integral part of their respective national movements; their goal, therefore, is self-determination and national sovereignty, not cultural and communal autonomy.

The unique complexity of the Jerusalem problem is that it is a political issue compounded by two secondary, related questions: those of the holy places and of municipal ethnic preeminence. The question of who is "sovereign" in Jerusalem is decisive yet not exclusive. Ethnic and religious disputes would endure even if a formula for an overall political control were found. But those secondary issues cannot be successfully handled until the major issue is resolved.

A common notion is that one can isolate the Jerusalem question from the general conflict over Palestine. It is argued that Jerusalem, being such a complex and unique issue, should be dealt with only after all other outstanding problems have been solved. This is a sound tactical approach, but it should not be construed that there can be a political solution to Jerusalem that will be basically different from the political solution to the Palestine question. The dispute is between Israelis and Palestinians, and a solution must be found by those directly involved in it. All other schemes, such as internationalization or extraterritoriality, will be rejected by both sides or will not endure.

In devising political solutions for Jerusalem, one is tempted to regard it as a border dispute. Such disputes are usually solved by drawing demarcation lines that define absolute political jurisdictions. Absolute sovereignty in Jerusalem is impossible, and both sides clearly understand that, as manifested by the universal agreement to keep the physical unity of the city. The Israelis insist on exclusive political control over the united city but recognize that they must limit their control, at least as far as the holy places and local autonomy of the Arab inhabitants are concerned. The Arabs, insisting on the political partition of Jerusalem, are nevertheless suggesting a united municipality, which indicates willingness to restrict their control.

As long as the conflicting parties maintain their subjective perceptions of the reality and remain entrenched in their unyielding positions, the conflict will remain insoluble.

Those who belong to the "ultimate solution" school dismiss partisan perceptions as childish misconceptions. The issues are for them real, objective, and quantifiable; therefore they can be solved. If the parties will not listen to reason, external pressure should be applied. Such attempts at this stage of the conflict are not only doomed to failure, they are counterproductive.

It is a well-known fact that when a conflict escalates, perceptions become stereotyped, every move is interpreted as a menace, views that do not fit the established political line are rejected, those who try to present alternatives are considered traitors, and moderates are intimidated and fall silent. Under such circumstances, any comprehensive plan will be regarded as a hostile act and will exacerbate the conflict even further.

A different approach is now sorely needed. It should be a gradual process in the course of which the parties will be called upon to make only those decisions that seem to them reasonable within the framework of their perceptions. They should be faced with a series of clear and legitimate choices, each involving specific action that they are capable of making and which will render desirable results. A choice, presented now, between Jerusalem and peace is clearly illegitimate in the eyes of the Israelis and will be rejected. A choice between further deterioration of internal security or some concessions to the local inhabitants would seem fair.

Bearing in mind the nature of the Jerusalem question, we all know that at some point the equation "Jerusalem = Peace" will be posed for a solution. A gradual approach would prepare the parties to regard it as a legitimate choice. By then peace should assume such a positive value that its preservation will create enough incentive to seek alternative arrangements for Jerusalem. These arrangements can be at the same time flexible and nevertheless safeguard the basic needs of both communities in the city.

5

Shibboleth

The mobilization order was delivered to me one evening in the last week of May 1967 while I was proofreading a manuscript on Crusader sites in the Holy Land due to be published that fall.

When I began the project I decided not to rely on written material and instead base the study on personal field surveys. There was a serious snag in that approach: the Crusader Kingdom of Jerusalem encompassed at its peak a much larger area than pre-1967 Israel. It ruled over South Lebanon, the Golan Heights, Moab and Edom in Trans-Jordan, and of course the West Bank. Important sites—notably the Old City of Jerusalem, but also Bethlehem, Sabastiya, Tyre, Sidon, Kerak, and Beaufort—were all inaccessible to me. I knew them by heart, had studied their ground plans and their dramatic history, but couldn't visit them, so I did not dare write about them.

I gave the manuscript to a friend and entrusted him with getting it to press. I had a premonition that I would be killed in the war. Two weeks later, after the Six-Day War, I asked the publisher for a postponement. My missing Crusader sites were suddenly within my reach. I could explore the Church of the Holy Sepulchre, the cloister of the Church of the Redeemer, St. Catherine in Sinai and in Bethlehem, St. John on the Jordan, even Coral Island off Eilat on the Red Sea—the base of the notorious pirate Renault de Châtillon. Others went

131

on pilgrimages to the Tombs of the Patriarchs, to Shiloh, Bethel, and Anathoth. I surveyed castles, nunneries, sugar mills, and ruined churches with my son Eyal, aged ten, holding the measuring tape.

It was a bizarre impulse for a Jew to study the material remains of those who massacred Jewish communities in Europe before embarking on their crusade to deliver the Holy Sepulchre from the infidel, a strange way to reacquaint myself with provinces of my ancestral homeland inaccessible for nineteen years. Yet this is my scholarly discipline, and in a peculiar way my reference point for the landscape of *moledet*.

Fifteen years later I understood the relationship of Crusader sites to *moledet*. In 1982 Israel invaded Lebanon. Again I was mobilized, this time as a lecturer, instructing the troops on the history of Lebanon. Again Crusader sites lured me. I ran from Tyre to Château de Mer in Sidon, from Tibnin to Beaufort. I wrote one article in a magazine, then felt disgusted with myself. I felt like a looter, breaking into the home of defenseless aliens and taking away their property. Lebanese ruins were indeed my castles, but not my *moledet*. In my provincial way I am interested only in ruins situated in my own homeland. I refused repeated requests to guide people to the Lebanese sites. I had no business in Lebanon—that was easy to understand. The West Bank, however, is an entirely different matter.

I traveled often, before 1948, with my father to Bethlehem, Hebron, and the Dead Sea. I listened to his stories about hikes in the wilderness of Judah; my uncles traveled every day to work in the potash factory on the Dead Sea, destroyed by the Jordanians in 1948. I remembered vividly the horror stories of attacks on Jewish convoys trying to bring supplies to the besieged settlements in the Hebron mountains during the War of Independence. One afternoon in January 1948 I played basketball at school with a group of Haganah fighters. Two days later they were dead. They had attempted to break the siege of the Jewish Etzion Bloc by using mountain paths at night. An Arab shepherd discovered them, and the whole force, thirty-five strong, perished after a fierce battle.

It was with this emotional load that in 1967 I crossed the minefields on the Bethlehem road and drove southward with my unit. We reached the ruined Kibbutz Kfar Etzion, converted into a Jordanian army camp, but continued immediately to nearby Hebron. We had an old score to settle there. In 1929 the Jewish community of that ancient town was massacred by the Arabs. The inhabitants knew what was on our minds and therefore were very careful not to give us any excuse. The whole city seemed empty, and large white flags were displayed on every house. We drove straight to the Tombs of the Patriarchs. There we ceremoniously climbed the steps leading to the magnificent Herodian structure, counting loudly each step. When we reached the seventh we shouted, "Eight, nine, ten . . ." until we reached the main gate. Jews were never allowed to climb beyond the seventh step, and there could only peer through the narrow slit to the dark vaults where their ancestors lie buried. Standing there, I remembered my previous visit, in 1944. My father was guiding a group of Jewish soldiers of the British Army. An Arab approached my father and handed him a crumpled piece of paper. It was an official letter of the Jewish community council of Hebron, dated 1929, recommending the bearer as an "honest and knowledgeable guide for Jewish sites in Hebron." I remembered how a Jewish soldier slapped the Arab and shouted: "How dare you show us this letter signed by those whom you murdered?"

For us standing in the cave of Machpelah the West Bank story did not start in 1967. For many it had started thirty-seven hundred years before, when Abraham bought the double cave from Ephron the Hittite. For my generation and for those older than we, the partition of Palestine caused by the 1948 war no longer existed. Indeed the nineteen years of partition were erased from our memory the moment we set foot in Bethlehem, reached the river Jordan, climbed Mount Gerizim. We returned to the parts of our *moledet* that were close to us, to the actual scenes of the historic events that had made the Jews into a nation. The profound emotional experience of the return affected everybody, atheist and fundamentalist, liberal and conservative. Its political expression was the rapid change in the perception of the Six-Day War itself.

When Israel went to war with Egypt, Prime Minister Levi Eshkol transmitted an urgent message to King Hussein: "We are engaged in a defensive battle in the Egyptian sector, and we will initiate no action in the Jerusalem sector unless Jordan attacks us. If Jordan attacks Israel, we will assault her with all our forces." King Hussein admitted that he received the warning: "[Israel warned that] if we did not intervene, they would save us from consequences which otherwise were inevitable: but by that time we no longer had any choice. We were obliged to do everything to help our allies."

Once the lines were crossed and the area occupied, the war aims changed from those of a defensive war to a war of liberation. Moshe Dayan stated at the Western Wall: "We have returned to our most holy places; we have returned and we shall never leave them." A new conception took over that interpreted the Six-Day War as a direct extension of the 1948 war, taking care of "unfinished business." This is not surprising, since most leading Israeli statesmen who dealt with post-1967 national policies took part in pre- and post-1948 major political and military decisions: Moshe Dayan was the military commander of Jerusalem in 1948; Yigal Allon, a member of the inner war council, was the commander of the Palmach elite military formation in 1948–49. In 1949 he submitted a plan to occupy the West Bank in a blitz operation, but it was turned down by Ben-Gurion; Menachem Begin, a minister without portfolio in 1967, tabled a bill in 1949 that declared the "Temple Mount, the Western Wall and all the Mandatory municipal boundary"—which were then occupied by Jordan—as parts of united Jerusalem, the capital of Israel. All these leaders perceived their actions after 1967 as a direct continuation of their actions in the 1948 war. Michael Brecher, who studied the foreign policy decisions of Israel, shows that as crucial a decision as the annexation of East Jerusalem in 1967 was, it was a mere tactical decision, "the consummation" of the "initial high-level policy decision to assert Israel's overall claim to the city" taken in 1948. Indeed, the government of Israel had offered in June 1967 to withdraw from the territories in return for peace, and top experts were convened to consider the future of the West Bank following an Israeli withdrawal, but the prevailing policy was Dayan's famous declaration that he was "waiting for a phone call from the Arabs." On June 13, 1967, he added: "We won't make any move. We are perfectly satisfied with what we have attained. If the Arabs want the situation changed, they should contact us." Even those experts who advocated a more active policy were captives of their preconceived ideas. They presented the same views they had put forward nineteen years earlier: some looked for a Palestinian solution; others saw the Kingdom of Jordan as the representative of the Palestinians; still others envisioned an Israeli-Palestinian-Hashemite confederation. It all remained theoretical, and in the meantime the occupation brought about a slow but steady reevaluation of its significance. The perception of the West Bank and Gaza as "liberated territories" spread from hypernationalistic to mainstream, moderate Israelis. Its symbolic expression is the change of formal definitions of the territories from "occupied West Bank" to "administrated Judea and Samaria," and then simply to the "areas of Judea and Samaria."

More significant, however, is the extension of traditional Labor-Zionist doctrines of settlement to the occupied territories and the creation of physical faits accomplis to achieve national, political, and military objectives. Post-1967 Labor leaders followed Ben-Gurion's maxim of 1949: "Only agricultural settlements along the borders will serve as a reliable barrier to defend the state from attacks: a living, working, and creative human wall would defend our boundaries." Moshe Dayan stated in 1971: "The settlement is the most important and most significant element in creating political facts." Yigal Allon's famous geostrategic plan, submitted to the Israeli cabinet less than a month after the war, in July 1967, used the same terminology: security borders must coincide with political borders, and borders become political only if Jewish settlements exist along their length.

Israeli youth, members of kibbutz-oriented movements, were called upon to continue the Labor-Zionist pioneering enterprise. Settling in the desert of Jericho and on the foothills bordering the Palestinian-populated highland region, they perceived themselves as following in the footsteps of the early pioneers. "Settlement in empty areas" had been accepted by moderate, liberal Israelis as a legitimate extension of the Zionist ethos. Many opposed settlements in heavily populated Palestinian areas but only out of self-interest: it would entail the absorption of a large Arab population, which would endanger the Jewish character of the state. Some believed that settlement activity was not antithetical to a political solution, for the areas outside the Allon Plan provided ample space for territorial compromise. Yet once Zionist action had been legitimized and the principle established, it would soon be impossible to set limits on the extent of the area to which it applied. Security considerations and perceptions of what Arabs should accept as fair compromise were flexible and ever changing. The Allon Plan itself expanded to encompass even larger areas. When religious fundamentalists succeeded in establishing themselves near Hebron, the Allon Plan was duly modified to include that area. Other Labor ministers had their own political and security notions, and put forward settlement plans. A dovish minister of housing suggested in 1974 a plan for "thickening Jerusalem." He argued that Israel would be able to retain only the metropolitan area of Jerusalem and that all other West Bank regions would ultimately be handed back to Jordan. He proposed, therefore, to establish satellite towns within a radius of ten to fifteen miles from Jerusalem and commenced, with the consent of the government, to implement his plan. A third minister argued in 1976 that security and political considerations required that Israel's narrow "waist" between Tel Aviv and Hadera—a mere twelve miles wide—be expanded; a new settlement region was duly opened in 1976. I followed the decision-making process closely. As head of the Jerusalem planning commission I participated in many top-level sessions and tours, during which major, irreversible planning decisions were taken. One day in the fall of 1974 we were asked to assemble at the heliport near the prime minister's office. A distinguished group of ministers, headed by the prime minister himself, boarded the huge air force helicopter. We took off, encircled the old city, and landed on the bare hill off the Jericho highway, five miles from Jerusalem's eastern outskirts. The object of the exercise was to determine the location of a new industrial estate. As planners spread maps and began their explanations, I watched the politicians. They were clearly disinterested in professional details. For them the issue was purely political; they felt that they were determining the future boundaries of Israel. The debate among them revolved around the question of whether by establishing an industrial area they were violating the geostrategic principle of the Allon Plan, which sought to keep open an "Arab corridor" from the river Jordan to Jerusalem. Others emphasized the strategic importance of the Jerusalem-Jericho axis, and the tactical qualities of this or that particular hill. Urban growth, pollution, landscape, dispersal of population, accessibility, and other urban matters seemed secondary, even petty. The ministers decided that an industrial area was not a settlement and therefore did not violate the Allon Plan. The issue was not over. A couple of months later the government was asked to decide on a "work camp" near the industrial area. By majority vote the cabinet decided to approve it, provided that it would not be turned into a permanent settlement. Everybody knew, however, that the "camp" was in fact a nucleus for an urban center, for the Ministry of Housing was busy planning it. Less than ten years later the "work camp" is a thriving, fast-growing town of ten thousand people.

When Labor fell from power in 1977, not less than 40 percent of the West Bank landmass was designated as settlement areas ultimately to be incorporated into Israel proper. The remaining area was perceived as sufficient to induce sensible Arabs to accept this as "a fair territorial compromise." Labor leaders believed that their policies in the West Bank were consistent with their ideology: they adhered to their historic acceptance of the partition of Palestine, and also to the Zionist conception of perpetual revolution and "reclaiming of the land." In effect, however, their policies proved to undermine their traditional, pragmatic doctrine and produced insoluble ideological contradictions. The relevance of the Zionist ethos to the occupied territories, the application of the old pioneering ideology to West Bank settlements, would supply the imprimatur of legitimacy to their bitter political and ideological opponents. The seemingly pragmatic, nondoctrinaire policy, which avoided extreme religious and historical claims, would legitimize Likud's nationalist-fundamentalist ideology.

The bankruptcy of Labor did not become apparent as long as they remained in power and formulated national policies. But once they lost power and Likud assumed the role of national leadership, it could exploit Labor's extension of the Zionist ethos to carry out its own policies of total annexation. Likud took over Labor's methods and symbols wholesale to initiate a massive settlement program in all parts of the West Bank. The precedent was established, and its gradual expansion was brought to its logical conclusion, or if one prefers, carried *ad absurdum*.

It is ironic that the dissident Revisionist stream of Zionism, of which Likud is a direct continuation, had adopted both the policies and the symbols of mainstream Labor-Zionism, which they always scorned. Revisionism believed in defining ultimate political objectives and advocated direct political and military action to attain them. Labor's constructivist, gradual doctrine formulated only intermediate, attainable political objectives and maintained that only concrete physical facts ("acre after acre, a goat and another goat") would bring Zionist goals within reach. Indeed, Labor believed its policy in the West Bank to be a continuation of the same doctrine, but they failed to appreciate that in the new context it would achieve the opposite result. The establishment of settlements had become the main vehicle for permanent annexation of the territories and of foreclosing political options. On Independence Day 1981, Ariel Sharon, then defense minister, ordered the establishment of fifteen NAHAL settlements in the West Bank. NAHAL is the acronym for a military formation established in 1949 to enable pioneering youth to combine military service with agrarian kibbutz life, preparing them to establish their own kibbutzim. NAHAL had been an ingenious concept, adapting pre-state voluntary *hagshama* to compulsory army service. Scores of NAHAL kibbutzim are strewn over the map of Israel and are an integral part of the Labor-Zionist ethos. The day a NAHAL group "ascends to the land," as the act of settlement is termed in Hebrew, is a day of reckoning. It signifies the realization of a dream, the culmination of years of preparation, a sign of maturity, the beginning of a new life based on social justice and idealism. The inauguration ceremony is a ritual by which the founding fathers are reincarnated. Imagine the havoc wreaked on the NAHAL groups and their parent organizations by Sharon's command. They were ordered to settle in locations unsuitable for permanent settlement, to be used mainly for propaganda. Their main task was to take possession of land confiscated from Palestinian farmers.

Sharon reacted to the angry objections of the youth organizations by stating that he was the competent authority to decide on security-settlement policies and was empowered to give orders to the army, NAHAL included. If they refuse to supply the groups, he might consider the liquidation of NAHAL. It was an impossible dilemma: if the youth organizations disobeyed, they would be disavowing the principle of respecting an order issued by a democratically constituted authority, turning their backs on the concept of *hagshama*, questioning the doctrine of the close settlement-security relationship, and risking the dissolution of NAHAL. If they concurred, they would become party to a policy they opposed.

On the appointed day, fifteen inauguration ceremonies took place on the sites chosen by Ariel Sharon. While flags were hoisted and youth groups stood at attention, hundreds of demonstrators, members of Peace Now who opposed the settlement policies of Likud, were driven away from the sites by tear gas. Many of the Peace Now demonstrators belonged to the same youth organization whose other members "ascended to the land" that day.

Likud had usurped Labor's Zionist methods, symbols, and institutions but had no use for the conceptual framework that sustained them. For Likud, settlement activities served only one purpose: securing title over the whole of Eretz Israel. All means were justified to that end: wholesale land confiscation, profiteering, destruction of nature reserves. Settlement, in any shape or form—mansions, luxurious villas, townships—and everywhere, even close to the old border, became a patriotic endeavor. Suburban estates have been recognized as legitimate "pioneering settlements" eligible for world Zionist financial support. Even the geostrategic significance of settlement had been altered. Likud strategists, unlike their Labor adversaries, estimated correctly that the future of the territories will be determined by the Israeli body politic rather than by external military or political pressure. Therefore they neglected the settlements along the cease-fire line and have developed settlements situated near the metropolitan areas of Jerusalem and Tel Aviv. Their strategy was aimed at creating internal political facts rather than geostrategic facts. The objective was to form a strong domestic lobby composed of settlers in the new suburbs or people with an economic interest in the West Bank. The suburban settlers need not hold with Likud ideology. But they will constitute an effective barrier to any political alternative advocating territorial compromise simply because of their desire to protect their investment and the higher quality of life they have attained.

The success of Likud strategy was already manifest by the 1984 elections. Across the "green line," Labor with its left-wing satellite parties gained only 14 percent of the vote. Its failure in suburban areas was even more conspicuous. In a typical suburb of Jerusalem, situated five miles from the city in the West Bank and inhabited by middle-class commuters, Labor got 373 votes and Likud 1239. The new settlement strategy had exacerbated Labor's predicament. A heated debate began on whether Labor-controlled firms should accept construction work in the new West Bank towns. Socialist youth movements conducted ideological discussions on the question of opening youth clubs in the new urban centers. Planners who objected to Likud's unlimited settlement policy refused to accept planning jobs in them, only to remain unemployed, as 70 percent of all planning jobs in Israel were in the occupied territories. Peace Now activists who demonstrated against Likud settlements in a new suburb of Jerusalem were confronted by the residents, who shouted back, "We came here because we had no home in Jerusalem. We are not Likud supporters! Find us alternative housing or get out." It took Labor politicians, and indeed most observers, too long to realize that settlements are not merely dots on a map, serving geostrategic purposes, manned by soldiers. Their perception of the "human wall" had blinded them from seeing that settlements are living entities interacting with their environment and exposed to normal economic and urban market forces. The perception of the West Bank merely as a political and military issue caused them to view it as a totally separate entity, detached from Israel proper, like a colony beyond the sea. They failed to grasp the simple fact that the "green line" is an imaginary barrier and that the territories are separated from Israel merely by flimsy administrative and judicial arrangements. They believed that they could control forever the growth of settlements and build and dismantle them at will like military camps; they were oblivious to the fact that the West Bank is situated geographically in the middle of the country and that half of it should be regarded as catchment areas of Israel's two major metropolitan regions, Jerusalem and Tel Aviv. The law of connected vessels was bound to create a powerful spillover from the congested bursting metropolises to the relatively empty surroundings. It was only a matter of time before land profiteers exploited the tremendous difference in land values—reaching in some areas a ratio of ten to one—between lots situated a few yards west and east of the nonexistent "armistice line."

Likud strategists exploited the prohibitive land prices in the cities and the very small areas allotted for detached houses in Israel proper; they directed the centrifugal, suburban pulls to the West Bank. Unlike Labor, they had no particular interest in settlement of remote areas; their strategy was demographically rather than geopolitically oriented. In their official directives they stated: "The [new] settlement plan diverts the center of gravity away from the subsidized rural, communal villages [favored by Labor] to the demand forces [pushing] for semiurban settlements of high quality of life in high market-demand zones."

Indeed, they filled the West Bank with scores of additional dots in areas termed "low-demand areas" and corresponding to the densely populated Palestinian highland region. The objective of these settlements was defined thus: ". . . reducing to the minimum the possibility for the development of another Arab state in these regions. It would be difficult for the minority population to form a territorial continuity and political unity when it is fragmented by Jewish settlements." In these areas Gush Emunim established its nuclei of a new society, based on monopolizing the environment and terrorizing the Palestinian population. Yet these settlements remained, with few exceptions, small and underpopulated. The ideologically motivated settlers required to inhabit these remote regions were in short supply. Gush Emunim could mobilize thousands for demonstrations, hundreds to "ascend the land," but only scores to stay permanently. Even those who stayed are unable to earn a living on site. Many keep their working places in the city and commute every day. Most settlers, however, earn their living as state and Zionist agencies' employees, providing services to their small, artificial communities. They enjoy very high standards of services. Schools of fifteen to twenty pupils have a full complement of teachers teaching three or four pupils per class. The government must pump in enormous resources to keep these expensive political demonstrations afloat, and the pace is maintained or accelerated as the external or internal political situation demands. Traditionally, before elections to the Knesset, a "settlement operation" is carried out: huge trucks, carrying a dozen prefabricated houses reach a site, traveling on a dirt road opened the day before by bulldozers; cranes unload the houses; workers connect them to a generator; a platform is constructed, and a public-address system installed. In the late afternoon a minister with his retinue arrives, a group of kindergarten children welcome him with flowers and songs, the flag is hoisted and the minister speaks, then he boards his limousine and departs. A few minutes after him most settlers leave too. It will be months until the site is ready for permanent settlement, but the political fact is created and another dot, usually sporting a ringing, biblical name, is added to the map.

More than two thirds of the West Bank settlements are ghost towns, and their growth potential is very low. The remaining one third, however, is an entirely different story. In areas situated within a range of thirty to forty minutes' driving time from Jerusalem and Tel Aviv, thousands of detached, semidetached, and apartment houses are under construction. Access roads are paved to allow easy and fast commuting between the metropolises and the settlements. Industrial estates are built to accommodate factories moving out from zones in the cities that become residential. Middle-class Israelis are moving out to the territories to realize the suburban dream of a house and a bit of lawn. They flee from tiny apartments in the stifling, polluted city center to the heavily subsidized new housing estates. Crossing the invisible "green line" to the West Bank, they assume a patriotic posture and become pioneers. Wherever they settle they carry with them the Israeli administrative, political, judicial, and welfare systems. They move, ostensibly, out of Israeli territory (as the West Bank is not officially annexed) and should be under the jurisdiction of Jordanian law, but this "anomaly" is not taken seriously. A steady process of abolishing the legal difference between the status of the settlers in the West Bank and ordinary Israeli citizens is in its final stages. A legal device unique in modern jurisprudence is used to "annex" the Israeli settlers while effectively excluding the Palestinians and without officially incorporating the territories. Israeli laws and "emergency regulations" are extended to encompass Israeli settlers *ad personam*. The Israeli system is applied only to Jews or, in the euphemistic language of the law, to those "entitled to immigrate to Israel under the 'Law of Return, 1950.' " This personal and ethnic legal arrangement is not new in the Middle East. It is a revival of the old system of capitulations under which European residents of the Ottoman Empire were immune from local, "native" laws. They remained under the jurisdiction of the "civilized" codes of the West and of the local consular agents representing their respective countries. The principle of territorial jurisdiction basic to modern states is violated, but it is only a legal expression of the intentional blotting-out of the "green line" marking the boundary between the territories and Israel proper. It is also a direct consequence of the spreading out of Israeli suburbanites to dormitory communities. When Jewish housewives in the new suburbs complained that Israeli appliance service companies refused to service their washing machines because the owners reside "outside Israel," the Ministry of Trade and Industry issued an "emergency regulation" that extended the insurance obligation for appliances to Jewish settlements in the territories. The process becomes almost mechanical and is perceived as apolitical, meant to solve problems arising from the exigencies of everyday life. As in other urban processes, once the floodgates are lifted, a dynamic adjustment to a new situation creates almost inexorably further entanglement. It creates further complications for those who object to the policies of integration and puts them in an untenable position. When the regulations *ad personam* were debated before a Knesset committee, a dovish member objected, stating that

"it is annexation in disguise." A hawkish Likud member re-
torted, "What do you want—that Israeli settlers will evade
income tax? That they will be unable to earn a living? Must
you conduct your political battles on the backs of individuals?" The dove could not find an answer.

Yet "rectifying judicial anomalies" for Israeli individual
settlers was not sufficient. Their communal status had to be
equalized to that of other Israeli communities. They could not
have remained under the "primitive" municipal and administrative system of the territories, fit only for the "locals." The
government, therefore, created a new, independent, elected,
self-governing administrative and judicial system of Jewish
regional and local councils. These councils became the chan-
nel through which the Israeli authorities provide state services to the settlements. Their budgets are incorporated in the
general budgets of Israeli civilian ministries with standards
identical to those in Israel proper or even more generous. Of
course these standards apply only to Jewish settlers. Arabs
are entitled only to what the military government sees fit to
provide under the strict budgetary constraints of the Ministry
of Defense. The dual system is not confined to Israeli individuals or Israeli communities. The whole West Bank is operating
under a dual administrative system, one for Jews, one for
Arabs.

As one leaves Jerusalem's northern municipal border, one
is confronted with a prominent sign: WELCOME TO MATEI BIN-
YAMIN REGIONAL COUNCIL. A few yards up the road one enters
the Palestinian town of al-Bira. A stranger would assume
that al-Bira is under the jurisdiction of the Matei Bin-
yamin Council, but he would be wrong. That sign is meant for
Israelis only, which is why it is written only in Hebrew. It
signifies for Israelis that they are now under the jurisdiction
of an Israeli authority operating de facto under Israeli laws,
separate from the military government jurisdiction and from
its administrative division that apply only to the "locals." The
jurisdictional separation is achieved by an ingenious method.
The West Bank is divided into "general areas." Within these

general areas, noncontiguous patches of Israeli jurisdictional areas are delineated that include the planned (not just existing) areas of Jewish settlement and all areas considered as Israeli state land. The areas between these patches are under the jurisdiction of the military government. In these areas are Arab towns and villages with twenty times the number of inhabitants of the Jewish settlements. The size of the Arab population does not hinder the Israeli regional councils from monopolizing the environment and planning land-use zones, roads, and nature reserves, and implementing these plans with the assistance of the military government. This dual, ethnically segregated system is the inevitable consequence of a legal framework based on a double personal standard. Its persistence is not perceived in Israel as reprehensible but rather as expedient "for the duration."

Israel's new West Bank suburbanites travel every morning to their usual place of work in the city center. A couple of hours before them, other commuters use the same newly constructed roads to reach the same destination. The two waves of commuters never meet, neither on the road, nor in the city, not even when they return home: they belong to different worlds, one Israeli, the other Palestinian. The Israelis are middle-class professionals, office workers, or small entrepreneurs; the Palestinians are Israel's *Gastarbeiter*, its migratory proletariat. Almost half of the West Bank's breadwinners wake up at dawn, assemble in their village squares, board a fleet of buses, trucks, taxis, and pickups, and travel to the big city. Half of them—some fifty thousand—are "officially employed," supplied to the Israeli market by government "labor exchanges." They are the lucky ones; their minimum wages are state controlled, and working conditions are officially equal to those of Israeli workers. The other half are "illegals." Many of them assemble every morning in specially designated areas on the outskirts of Israeli towns, termed in local jargon as "slave markets," and wait. Israeli bosses pick some of them up for temporary jobs, while others return home unemployed. An elaborate, and illegal, system of recruitment is organized by Palestinian labor contractors who supply thousands of workers for underpaid, temporary jobs. Palestinian workers make up more than 5 percent of the Israeli work force, and their effect in the manual and menial sectors is significant. They amount to one third of the workers in construction and constitute a majority of unskilled laborers on actual construction sites. The true social significance of Palestinian labor is revealed, however, in sectors defined in the dry official jargon as "other branches." These are the restaurant dishwashers, gas station attendants, hotel cleaning crews, garbage collectors, and holders of other low-wage, low-status jobs. In these jobs Arab laborers are the overwhelming majority. One finds them in the entertainment districts, hanging on to garbage trucks, watering the gardens. Many of them are high school graduates, fathers of large families who can manage to return home only once a fortnight. They find shelter in mini-shantytowns sprouting on beaches, or in restaurant storage areas locked by the proprietors for the night. They are frequently harassed by the police, for their stay overnight in Israel is illegal.

The Israeli public realizes their presence only when they are absent. During the Muslim high holidays of 'Id al-Fitr and 'Id-al Adha, all garbage collection ceases and restaurant service is slow. Occasionally dehumanization assumes ugly proportions. When an entire garbage collection crew of Palestinians perished in a road accident, the mayor of the Israeli city who employed them issued an official notice asking the residents to refrain temporarily from throwing out garbage, "due to an accident." That was all.

Indifference to human dignity, blatant discrimination, and ethnocentrist sentiments characterize not only general attitudes. The institutional treatment of Palestinian laborers is indicative of the underlying communal norms. "Legal" laborers, supposedly protected by state agencies and trade unions, are institutionally discriminated against and suffer from lack of concern for their basic needs. The declared policy of the government is equal wages for equal work. But this policy was established in order to avoid giving Palestinian laborers an advantage over Israeli workers: that of being cheaper. The cost to the employer is equal, but the rights of the Palestinians are not. Basic daily wages are equal—but only Palestinians remain untenured. They are generally not entitled to monthly wages, sick days, vacations, bonuses, severance pay, seniority, and other fringe benefits that their Jewish coworkers are. But the major element of discrimination is in social security payment, pension allowances, and medical insurance. Although 20 percent of a worker's gross pay is transferred by the employer to the government for social security, the Palestinian laborer does not benefit from it. The enormous sums deducted since 1967 never reached the National Insurance Institute. They are transferred directly to the Treasury and kept there "until the future of the territories is determined." Then, according to Israeli officials, "the negotiating parties will decide on its disposition." In the meantime, Palestinian laborers have to make do without old-age allowance, child allowance, general disability allowance, unemployment, and wage compensation. The monies deducted from their wages, now huge sums accumulated over two decades, are not used to guarantee their future. They should instead be regarded as a sort of occupation tax, an added drain on meager Palestinian resources. Economists debate the impact of Palestinian labor on the Israeli economy. Most emphasize its marginal importance, given its low participation ratio (5 percent) in the total labor force. Some experts indicate also its negative impact on the economy: the sudden supply of unskilled, low-wage laborers enabled unproductive, labor-intensive branches to prosper and eliminated the need for mechanization and higher efficiency. It is fashionable to dismiss Palestinian labor and its unpleasant effects as marginal and easy to be terminated by Israeli withdrawal from the territories. Indeed, such perceptions prevail among trade union leaders and Labor party doves, who refuse to grasp the pervasiveness of the phenomenon and to deal with it lest it forge a permanent link between the territories and Israel, and thus "annex" them.

When in 1967–68 the government suggested to the Histadrut, the General Federation of Israeli Labor, that they should assume responsibility for Palestinian labor, the dovish leadership refused to deal with the issue. This would amount to annexation, they argued, and refused to manage even the enormous social payments deducted from the Palestinians, including medical care, which is supplied exclusively by the Histadrut. The government, then composed of Labor ministers, decided, therefore, to manage Palestinian labor through a governmental agency on a temporary basis. This was consistent with the general political approach "to decide not to decide" on the future of the territories, thus leaving options open for a political compromise.

Paradoxically, the institutional discrimination is derived from moderate, dovish political perceptions rather than from a discriminatory ideology. Yet the irony runs even deeper. Labor party perceptions of Palestinian labor should be seen in the context of the ethos of *avoda ivrit* (literally, "Hebrew labor"), a fundamental concept of traditional Zionist philosophy. Labor-Zionism believed in social redemption of the Diaspora Jew through manual, agricultural work. They wanted to rectify the inverted Jewish occupational pyramid composed of a few productive persons and an overwhelming majority of middlemen, peddlers, and intellectuals: in Palestine, Jews must become self-sufficient and do all physical work by themselves, including the most menial. *Avoda ivrit* was essential at the time to prevent the rise of a colonial society consisting of Jewish masters and Arab peons. Labor leaders in the Thirties waged an uncompromising and aggressive struggle against Jewish orange grove owners who used cheap Arab labor, and they fought the Arab laborers themselves. Mainstream Labor leadership closed Jewish trade unions to Arab workers. Attempts of Jewish left-wing groups to create binational cells were short-lived. *Avoda ivrit* was rampant with ideological inconsistencies as internationalism clashed with ethnocentrism. One could argue, however, that under the prevailing conditions it was the least of all evils.

Avoda ivrit created the economic and social basis on which the Jewish state was built. It also provided a belief system that insulated the Zionists from objective reality, and thus became a myth. This myth, combined with the myth of settlement, was perceived as everlasting and therefore valid in the context of post-1967 conditions. The absorption after the war of tens of thousands of unemployed Palestinians was perceived as a temporary expediency, a necessary evil that should not be allowed to endure. The continued employment of Arabs in construction, and especially in agriculture, had been perceived as undermining the very foundation of the Zionist enterprise, as Jews once again resumed the Diaspora occupational structure of the "inverted pyramid." Unable to control the forces they had unleashed so casually, Labor dismissed them as temporary. Labor apologists found consolation in devising comprehensive political solutions that would free them from the Palestinian presence in their midst: in a homogeneous Jewish state, all labor will be *avoda ivrit*, and the myth would remain untarnished. In the meantime, deliberate inaction seemed appropriate. Yet institutional indifference exacerbated discriminatory attitudes among the public and legitimized inequities. Moreover, the Israeli working class, predominantly Sephardim, sensed the hypocrisy: those who preach manual labor are middle-class, affluent Ashkenazim. What *avoda ivrit* really means, argue the Sephardim, is that *they* would return to the low-status, low-wage branches that they occupied before abandoning them to the Palestinians. Amos Oz captured that sentiment in Beth Shemesh: "What did they bring my parents to Israel for? . . . You didn't have Arabs then, so you needed our parents to do your cleaning and be your servants and your laborers. . . . If they give back the territories, the Arabs will stop coming to work, and then and there you'll put us back into the dead-end jobs like before.

... Look at my daughter: she works in a bank now, and every evening an Arab comes to clean the building. All you want is to dump her from the bank into some textile factory, or have her wash the floors instead of the Arab. That's why we hate you here."

When in 1984 the economic crisis created pockets of unemployment, thousands of Jews refused to accept jobs requiring manual work, claiming that "these are jobs for Arabs"—and lost their unemployment allowances.

The fact that Oriental Jews express more hostility toward Arabs than do Ashkenazi Jews is well known and amply documented. There are perceptual, cultural, and socioeconomic explanations for that phenomenon: Oriental Jews want to settle the score with the Arabs for the centuries of humiliation in the Arab countries and Arabs serve as "scapegoats" for lower-class, deprived Oriental Jews. Yet what is most pertinent in the present context is that Oriental Jews need the Arabs underneath them on the social ladder: they seek to maintain their superior status as belonging to the dominant Jewish group. As the man from Beth Shemesh told Oz, "If for no other reason, we won't let you give back the territories. Not to mention the rights we have from the Bible, or security. ... As long as Begin's in power," said the man, "my daughter's secure at the bank." But it was not Begin who initiated institutional discrimination. Labor politicians, purporting to "keep options open" and to adhere to lofty Zionist, anticolonialist ideals have created almost absentmindedly a system that conforms to classic colonial models. The system relies, paradoxically, *not* on organized state discrimination but rather on institutional neglect. Labor leaders refused, out of ideological paralysis and lack of direction, to transform it. Only political willpower was needed to organize Palestinian labor, represent them, and fight for their rights. But the willpower was missing, dissipated by ideological contradiction. The deplorable situation was conveniently blamed on the prevailing Likud political culture. But in any case, how could the situation be engaged when the angry men of Beth Shemesh and their peers, representing half of Israel's population, can legitimize their attitudes by pointing at Jewish union leaders condoning blatant inequities? In the meantime, a Palestinian ethnic class becomes an integral part of the Israeli system, occupying the lowest rung of the social ladder and destined to remain there, because this satisfies the deep-seated needs of deprived Israelis, without whom no change can be effected.

I have described at some length two unrelated phenomena: Israel's suburban sprawl and Palestinian migratory labor. Both have a profound impact on spatial, economic, social, and psychological interaction between Israelis and Palestinians. Both have already created internal Israeli political attitudes that may be detrimental to attempts at changing the status quo, and definitely push for further entanglement. Both processes illustrate how integrative processes, based on the release of objective forces, can become pervasive and develop much further than had been intended by those who so casually set them in motion. Most decisions concerning the occupied territories were made assuming that they were only temporary measures, the occupation itself being provisional, and options must remain open. Like most ad hoc decisions, they were inconsistent, pragmatic, and unrelated. It would perhaps be unfair to blame those who made them for what eventually came to pass, except that they themselves perceived them in a broader, historical context, and in doing so, granted them everlasting legitimacy. They may wash their hands of the outcome, but the fact that even when the full meaning of the consequences was revealed they did not openly repudiate them, indicates acquiescence or at least indifference.

Consider the issue of land acquisition in the territories. The Israeli-Palestinian struggle is encapsulated in the scramble for space. As we have seen earlier, it was land that the Zionist movement sought to liberate in order to create on it physical faits accomplis. The occupation of the West Bank was perceived as a direct continuation of the Zionist enterprise. The policies of "land reclamation" had been, therefore, vigorously pursued ever since the Six-Day War.

The Labor government, soon after the occupation, commenced to seize land in the territories. Operating by the well-learned methods of 1948, the government first appropriated "absentee" property and Jordanian government property. Although one fifth of the West Bank population left the area and migrated to Jordan, somewhat less than 8 percent of the land was abandoned, since most 1967 refugees were impoverished 1948 refugees. Israeli officials, anticipating wholesale abandonment of property as happened after the 1948 war, were disappointed. Moreover, the military government under Moshe Dayan imposed a very liberal policy on the land-hungry "Custodian of Absentee Property." The greater part of the area declared abandoned was given back to relatives of the absentees and therefore could not be used by the authorities. In the Jordan valley, however, absentee property was not returned and was instead leased to Israeli settlements established there according to the Allon Plan. Jordanian government property consisted mainly of army camps and large tracts of rocky hills located in remote areas. Israel occupied all army camps but had no use for the scattered areas unsuitable for settlement. Vast areas were closed for military purposes, but most of it was desert or uncultivated. Cultivated areas were seized by means of requisition orders declaring the areas "required for essential and urgent military needs." These areas were then given to Israeli settlers. When Palestinian farmers petitioned the High Court of Justice, their petition was rejected. The High Court accepted Israeli government statements that "all Israeli settlements are an integral part of the Israeli Defense Force," hence handing over the area to civilian Israelis constituted "military needs." Although the areas thus seized caused hardship and much publicity, their actual size was small. But for the purposes of the modest, security-oriented settlement policy of Labor, it was sufficient. Indeed, lack of land for settlement was used by the Labor government as a pretext to curb settlement activity of right-wing groups in areas considered "outside the settlement map of Labor." The same cautious policy is manifested in

Labor land-purchase activities. The government issued in 1967 an order forbidding any land transaction without a written permit and refused permits to private corporations and Israeli individuals. A permit was granted only to the Jewish National Fund. In 1973 Moshe Dayan proposed to open the area for unlimited land speculation, but the government turned his proposal down. Labor governments believed that firm control over land would guarantee absolute control over settlement activities.

Yet the Labor settlement policy itself was not uniform. Hawkish elements pushed for opening new settlement areas and therefore needed more space. The Government Land Authority offered a solution. They suggested that the criteria that applied in Israel proper vis-à-vis the Arab population be implemented in the territories; instead of claiming land piecemeal through requisition orders, the government should turn the tables and view all land as national patrimony except what Arab villagers could prove as their own by valid title deeds or by actual cultivation. This was a bold suggestion, because it meant that the pretense of land requisition "for the duration" be dropped, and with it the basic perception of the occupation as a provisional situation. The government did not sanction that fundamental policy change, but land experts carried out a survey of all uncultivated lands anyway.

This came in handy when Likud came to power in 1977. The new policy of massive settlement and the building of urban centers in all parts of the West Bank required more ambitious methods of land acquisition than those of Labor. Likud also refused to hide behind military excuses or to acknowledge that territories are "occupied"; for them, they are "liberated." The new regime established formally that if an area is not registered in the name of a local owner, the assumption is that the area can be claimed as state land as long as it is not cultivated. Concomitantly the ban on private land purchase was lifted and a rush of land speculation began. Both measures enable the Israelis to lay claim to 40 percent of the total landmass of the West Bank and thus to facilitate unlimited

Jewish settlements. The new definition of state land had been accepted as a valid and correct norm. Labor opposition never opposed it, and land-alienation processes continue smoothly under a "national unity" coalition composed of Labor and Likud. The principle, once established and implemented, cannot be revoked, for it would mean the cancellation of land-seizure orders through which thousands of dunams were taken and leased to private Israelis who built their homes on them. To discontinue the process amounts to almost nothing, because it is almost complete, and sufficient land has been alienated to enable the settlement of a million settlers.

It is not difficult to trace present conditions back to the seventh day of the Six-Day War. To be sure, the legal basis, physical facilities, military and security doctrines, economic policies, and ideological argumentation were all initiated and developed during the decade of Labor-controlled administrations. But can one conclude from it that Labor and Likud policies are identical and their objectives the same? Here we must consider not just actions and their results but also intents and purposes. It is in this context that we find the difference.

The Six-Day War was not a war of aggression, and the West Bank was not occupied to realize an ideological objective or to fulfill expansionist urges. It was imposed upon a Labor government that wished to maintain the status quo established by mutual agreement in 1949. Admittedly war aims were changed, as we have seen, but even when Labor leaders used nationalistic rhetoric, this was balanced by pragmatic and cautious actions. The "decision not to decide" on the future of the territories and theoretical commitment to territorial compromise enabled them to live with the intrinsically temporary nature of a military government. Their actions could have been taken as conforming with international law concerning occupied territories. Some of their actions, especially their settlements, strongly implied that they intended to stay, but they were not taken deliberately to exclude or to prejudice any political solution or to foreclose any right. *It was an occupation with a bad conscience.* Labor was torn by unresolved contradictions between its nationalistic, security-oriented objectives and its humanistic-socialist values. Labor adhered to the Zionist ethos of reclaiming the land but shrank from the inevitable consequence—which it abhorred—of subjugating the people living on it. In its distress, Labor looked for "Jordanian options," which basically meant to externalize the Palestinian problem by offering others the job of subjugating them. Their unresolved internal contradictions, exacerbated by the total Arab rejection of any compromise, caused political and ideological paralysis. They increasingly, and in some matters absentmindedly, stumbled into a classical colonial situation about which they themselves had warned. The prolongation of the occupation blunted the feelings of bad conscience. As actually happens when a status quo is established, it becomes respectable.

Into this ideological limbo stepped Menachem Begin, Likud leader and chief ideologue. He was never torn by any ambivalent attitude toward the territories. His fundamental ideological principle had always been the territorial integrity of Palestine, as determined in 1919, consisting of the areas of Western Palestine and Trans-Jordan, and the creation of a Jewish sovereign state within these borders. He objected and fought against all partition plans since the creation of Trans-Jordan in 1922, through 1936 and 1947, to the armistice agreement with Jordan in 1949. Although never advocating launching an attack on Jordan to liberate the West Bank, he viewed the Six-Day War as a war of liberation.

His accession to power as Likud prime minister in 1977 created a new situation in the territories. Ideologically he could not have accepted even the implied admission that the territories were "occupied." Permanent control over the Land of Israel has been axiomatic for his government. From now on, all pretenses of temporary occupation were dropped, and the dominant purpose has become to settle the whole area in order to prevent the "repartition of Eretz Israel." For Begin to accept the river Jordan as a permanent boundary and to relinquish claims to Trans-Jordan was a painful compromise.

He signed the Camp David accord and evacuated the Sinai because of his perception that in return he was to be given a free hand in the West Bank; he also wanted to establish through the peace agreement with Egypt the sanctity of the borders of Palestine as established under the Mandate. Likud had no qualms about the fate of the Palestinian inhabitants. Unlike Labor, Likud always perceived the conflict as a life-and-death struggle between two movements whose aspirations could never be bridged. Due to their strong belief in the moral superiority of their national aspirations, they were ready to wage a ruthless war. Permanent subjugation of Palestinians had been considered an inevitable byproduct of their victory. *They were occupiers with a clear conscience.* The colonial situation did not cause them any misgivings. They welcomed it and did their utmost to perpetuate it, to exclude and foreclose any other option except permanent annexation, and of course to prejudge any other right.

The difference between Labor and Likud is therefore one of intents and purposes. The former wavered, torn between conflicting ideological imperatives, preferring indecision, and by being indecisive, keeping the options open. The latter was unequivocal and acted to make the inequities permanent. The realities created were identical, but for those who abhorred them, there was still a difference. There was a chance that once the full magnitude of the realities were know to Labor, they would overcome their hesitancies and stand firm against further deterioration.

This was on my mind when I began almost a decade ago to compile data on the changing conditions in the territories and to fit the data into a theoretical framework. When I had amassed sufficient empirical data I began, like all social scientists, to conceptualize it. I asked myself the simple question; Of what is Israeli occupation a "case"? Is it a classical occupation similar to U.S. occupation of Germany after the Second World War? Is it a colonial expansion? And if it is, is it similar to the British raj in India, or to the British presence in Kenya

or in Ireland? Is this an "Algerian case"? Is it a linear development of the 1947 condition? As I struggled with the data and
tried to conceptualize it into models, I realized that one cannot
understand objective realities without putting them in the
context of the perceptual framework of the forces that
brought them about. So I began asking another question: Of
what is the Israeli-Arab conflict a "case"? Is it a binational—
Israeli-Palestinian? Is it a West–Third World conflict? Is it
racial, plural, anticolonial, internal colonial? Is it all of those
combined?

I understood that all models I used are not value-free, for
apart from their diagnostic value, they possess an implicit or
explicit prescriptive significance; they are code words calling
for action. Reality is partly perception. In our situation there
are no objective data and no scientific models. Attitudes to
real facts are predetermined by perception, position, wishful
thinking. I knew that my own models, though mere analytical
instruments for approximating a chaotic reality, would be
criticized as being self-serving and rightfully so. I was not an
impartial onlooker; I had a clear position based on my own
value system: concern for human rights and dignity. Torn as
I am between my inner contradictions, I thought that there
are fundamental, universal norms that are irrefutable, and it
is against those that I must assess the situation, construct my
conceptualization, arrive at value judgments, and suggest
prescriptions.

Looking back, equipped with the wisdom of hindsight, I
must admit that some of my conclusions about Labor activities in the territories were premature and too rushed. The
dynamic process of creeping annexation, the attempt to gain
permanent control or to make permanent Israeli control more
easily attainable, was definitely there. But the evidence was
inconclusive. Some actions could have been interpreted as
implying ultimate annexation but not over the whole territory. Some actions have foreclosed rights and usurped powers
but could have been explained by security needs. The classic
though theoretical model of "belligerent occupation" as

defined in international conventions could still be applicable to the territories, admittedly with great difficulty. Other models have been offered, but the data supplied to support them were inconclusive enough to allow Israel the benefit of the doubt. Two years after Menachem Begin acceded to power, I realized that the model of military occupation, which assumes an intrinsically temporary condition, had become obsolete. A new model, defining Israeli interaction in its territories on a more permanent basis, was patently needed. I found a plethora of definitions, each with its emotional political and historical overtones, to describe the new condition. One definition, perhaps the least emotionally charged, is "pluralism." Sami Smooha sums up pluralism by stating that multiethnic societies are marked by cultural differences, structural segmentation and pervasive segregation, exceedingly disproportionate distribution of resources, asymmetric economic interdependence and political domination, vulnerability to instability, and violence. Another fitting model is the "colonial model": an external power occupies a foreign territory and establishes a coercive regime based on total subordination of the colony to the military, political, and economic interests of the colonial power. The external power permits or even encourages the settlement of its own civilians in the new colony. The settlers form a superior class, control a disproportionate part of the economy, and exploit the local population through their monopoly on political and military power. The settler society is characterized by spatial, social, and occupational segregation, as well as by racial prejudice. Colonial situations are typical to overseas territories of the imperial era. Postcolonial models of superordinate-subordinate relations, called "internal colonialism," emphasize that the colonial characteristics are not affected when the ties between the colonial mother country and the colony are severed. The role of the colonial white settler is assumed by an indigenous superior group and the "native" subordinate group retains its colonial status. Internal colonialism, however, resembles structural pluralism and is only a pseudoscientific political code word used by

Third World revolutionary movements as a call for action. Surveying the conditions in the territories, I could easily find all the elements specified as supporting the pluralist or the colonial models: total monopoly of Israelis over all political and military power, including the elimination of independent local municipal councils; usurpation of natural resources, mainly of land and water; asymmetric economic interdependence resulting in the transformation of the territories into a classic colonial model of a cheap source of unskilled labor and protected outlets for Israeli manufactured goods; separate judicial and administrative systems; spatial segregation of Israeli settlement from Palestinian towns and villages; violence perpetrated by Israeli vigilantes and Palestinian terrorists; a ban on political expression and on the use of Palestinian communal symbols; pervasive social stratification of superiors and inferiors.

The symptoms were identical, but I was intrigued by the question, Which case is it—pluralism or colonialism? It sounds very technical—one of those clinical hair-splitting devices used to gain comfortable distance from real life. Yet it is a useful distinction because it points to the core of the problem. Pluralism implies that the fundamental causes of the malaise are *internally* generated. Social and political inequities as well as instability in a plural society are caused by pervasive friction of groups residing in close proximity on one territory; by different cultural and social backgrounds of two different ethnic groups; a high level of respective political cohesiveness; and conflicting political aspirations caused by one ethnic group's struggle for control over the shared territory or for liberation from the other group's rule. The colonial situation, by contrast, is *externally* generated. It stems from the activity of external powers who occupy foreign territories overseas (or border theirs). Such colonial situations are terminated when the external power, whose locus is outside the area, in the "old" country, terminates its involvement voluntarily, or is forced to, and evacuates its army, followed by its settlers, while those remaining lose their superior status. To be sure, colonial situations may evolve into plural societies when the transplanted settlers manage to form a cohesive society powerful enough to survive on its own, following the departure of the parent colonial power. When the imperial powers formed colonies, they initiated a process that caused the indigenous population to detach itself from a larger ethnic group and develop a distinct national identity within the colonial borders. External powers may incite ethnic groups in their neighboring countries in order to achieve political objectives. These border conflicts cease when the external power decides to inflame them no longer.

By defining the core problem—external or internal—one may isolate the major issue from a host of secondary problems. If the major issue is identified as an externally generated conflict, external powers rather than local leadership should be approached. If, however, the conflict is internally generated, then it is organic and endemic and resistant to comprehensive surgical solutions.

My preconceived idea was that our conflict is externally generated, and therefore the situation in the territories resembles a colonial situation. These conceptions conformed with those of most observers. It seemed obvious: one state occupies a province, settles its own nationals, monopolizes its resources, and creates a colonial economic interdependence. What can be more colonial? Yet I began to wonder if the model is appropriate. The colonial model implies a distinct "mother country" whose seat of power, symbolized by the capital, is situated outside the colony. As an Israeli, I had no doubt that Jerusalem is that capital. But is it plausible that one part of Jerusalem—East Jerusalem—would be considered a colony? And if it is not, but thought of rather as an integral part of the "mother country," why not Bethlehem or Jericho? Why are inequality and instability in East Jerusalem perceived as internal (pluralistic) and the same pattern in neighboring Bethlehem perceived as external (colonial)?

Colonial situations are externally generated, but who are the external powers? One is Israel, but is it external? The other is Jordan, from whom the territory has been taken, but the Jordanians themselves were occupiers who established in the West Bank a colonial situation between 1948–1967 characterized by the same elements of economic exploitation and a hierarchy of superiors and inferiors no different than the Israelis. Colonial situations are terminated when the occupying power leaves the province. If the two external powers, Israel and Jordan, were to agree on an Israeli evacuation and a return to the *status quo ante bellum*, would the colonial situation cease to be?

The answer must be negative, because then Jordan would impose its own colonial situation. The destabilizing factor is clearly not the Jordanians, but the occupied people, namely the Palestinians. Can we define them as an external element? Where is their external power base? Where is their capital— Amman, Beirut, Jerusalem? Do they perceive the West Bank as a distinct province? Is the relationship between Israelis and Palestinians a colonial relationship like the French and Algerians, British and Kenyans? Or is it like Maronites and Shiites in Lebanon, Protestants and Catholics in Ulster? Would the conflict between them cease when external powers inflame it no more, or is it a result of an internally generated dispute for control over a shared territory? Is the post-1967 situation a novel condition, or is it rooted in the past? I began to realize that the colonial model is too simplistic and convenient. I thought that I could trace the perceptions of the conflict as externally generated to pre-1967 concepts.

As we have seen earlier, both Israelis and Palestinians perceived the other side as an extraneous element. The Israelis were viewed as white-settler foreigners and the Zionist entity as colonial. The Palestinians were perceived as squatters who emigrated from the Arab states. Both looked toward external powers for a solution: the Arabs to the U.S., Israel's "mother country" without which it cannot survive; the Israelis to the Arab states, to whom the Palestinians belong. Both refused to perceive their adversary as a legitimate national group and to define their strife as an internally generated binational conflict. The Israelis saw the Palestinians as a cultural, religious, or an ethnic minority. The Arabs viewed Zionism as a racist, exclusionary movement and the Jews as a religious group composed of "Arab Jews, euphemistically called Oriental, and non-Arab Jews [Ashkenazim] who dominate them." The denial is expressed by an Israeli writer thus: "There was never a Palestinian Arab nation . . . to the people as a whole, no such entity existed . . . those few who lived within its bounds may have had an affinity for their villages —for their clan—they were not conscious of any relationship to a land." Palestinian perception of Zionism was symmetrical as stated in the Palestinian National Convenant: "The claim of historical or spiritual links of the Jew to Palestine is not in accordance with historical facts. . . . Judaism, being a religion, is not an independent nationality with an identity of its own; Jews are also not one people but citizens of the country in which they reside."

The years of partition had reinforced, as we have seen, the exclusionary attitudes but did not change the basic perceptions of the conflicting parties about the integrity of the disputed land. There was no doubt about Palestinian feelings for "occupied Palestine," namely Israel. Israeli perceptions about the West Bank were initially submerged, but the emotional reaction to the occupation proved that for the majority of Israelis the acceptance of partition did not constitute a fundamental compromise with the Palestinians but was rather a phase in the realization of Zionist objectives. Most Israelis and Palestinians agreed, from their opposed perspectives, on the significance of the war and the occupation; both perceived it in the context of their hundred-year war. For the Palestinians, Israeli occupation of the West Bank was no more colonial than the occupation of the Galilee. For the Israelis, Bethlehem and Hebron were not "liberated" in a different fashion than, say, Jaffa and Acre. The "green line" separating the two areas did not survive long enough to become a psychological Strait of Gibraltar separating France from Algeria. The partition did not outlive the generation that actually fought the 1948 war, or their sons who were raised on the memories of Acre and Haifa, Bethel and Etzion. The war in 1948 was the end of one act in the tragedy, and the beginning of another. The curtain fell and rose again in 1967, but the drama was far from being over. The theme was unaltered, only the characters developed, and the tragedy was close to its denouement.

In the new act the two communities found themselves for the first time in their long history alone on the stage, with no intermediaries like the British or the Jordanians. The Israelis had to govern a population amounting to almost a third of their own, not merely a tiny Arab minority tucked in a remote area. The Palestinians had to confront personally and communally the "artificial Zionist entity," which to their surprise was robust and thriving. They realized that the Jews are here to stay, and that they don't take orders from anyone. The Israelis realized that unlike 1948, physical "externalization" or even conceptual elimination of a strong and cohesive Palestinian community was no longer possible. As Edward Said observed, "Two things are certain: the Jews of Israel will remain; the Palestinians will also remain."

Both sides had to relate to each other directly and began to realize that as much as their perceptions of the conflict as externally generated were justified in the past, they were not valid anymore. They sensed that the conflict could not be solved by force or coercion, but they could not extricate themselves from their petrified nationalistic ethos and were unable to formulate realistic policies. The Palestinians clung to their conception of "armed struggle" formulated in 1936 and believed in the creation of a sovereign Palestinian state in the territory of the British Mandate, which according to the Palestinian Covenant is "one integral territorial unit." Even those who were ready to accept a Palestinian state in the occupied territories insisted that it would be a mere territorial base for the perpetual revolution whose ultimate goal is "the return" to Haifa and Jaffa. They were mirror-imaged by the Likud, who took steps to ensure that Palestine would remain "one integral territorial unit" under Israeli control. The difference was that Likud possessed the power to achieve it, partially because Israelis feared that the Palestinians might be capable of achieving their own goals.

Opposing radical groups usually reinforce one another; they thrive on atavistic feelings of fear and revenge aroused by their mirror-image group. Both PLO and Likud offered an almost identical "solution" to the internal government of their "integral territorial unit"; the PLO called it Secular Democratic Palestine, and Menachem Begin suggested autonomy for the inhabitants. Both meant the elimination of the other group as a community and its fragmentation into powerless individuals living under the absolute tyranny of the only legitimate collective in the land—Palestinians or Israelis.

Yet with all their extremism and intransigence, both Likud and the PLO understood the nature of the conflict in which they were engaged. They perceived it as an internally generated strife to be decided on the soil of the land west of the Jordan and nowhere else. The PLO (or at least its mainstream faction) abandoned the antiimperialist, Nasserite illusion and concentrated on their historic adversary. Likud, on its part, eliminated the external conflict with Egypt and indeed was prepared to pay a heavy price for it by abandoning Sinai. The conflict shrank almost to its pre-1948 size.

Both sides refused to call their adversary by name and to define the conflict as internally generated, but their actions left no doubt. This much cannot be said about the Israeli moderates. Indeed a minority of Israelis and even fewer Palestinians drew conclusions diametrically opposed to those of the radicals. They also perceived the conflict as internally generated and advocated a fundamental compromise based on a symmetry between the two communities. They called for mutual recognition of national aspirations, which meant self-determination in two separate sovereign states sharing the land. This ideological, elitist, solution-oriented philosophy had failed to attract the general Israeli public because its message contradicted deep-seated exclusionary attitudes. As long as the radicals succeed in maintaining a psychological "state of siege," the chances for gaining wider support for this conciliatory approach seem very slim and their impact on events marginal.

The real tragic hero of the Jewish-Arab drama is Labor-Zionism. The movement that for three generations bore the full burden of Zionist-Arab policies found itself after 1967 a victim of its pragmatism, moderation, and inner contradiction, but primarily the victim of Arab hostility and extremism.

From its first steps in Palestine, the socialist-universalist stream of Zionism was unable to perceive the conflict as an internally generated clash of two national movements. They could not confront the stark reality that the realization of Zionist objectives must come at the expense of the Palestinians.

David Ben-Gurion, Labor-Zionism personified, expressed his dilemma in the twenties: "Zionism did not have the moral right to harm one single Arab child, even if it could realize all its aspirations at that price." Labor evaded the communal clash by depicting the conflict as an international class struggle where a Jewish proletariat fights Arab landowners disguised as nationalist leaders. When the true nature of the conflict began to emerge, Labor believed that Palestinian nationalism was backward, reactionary, and fascist, supported by ignorant peasants. Zionism would improve their living conditions and help develop their culture—until finally they would learn to accept the justice of the Jewish claim.

Their moderation and humanism compelled them, paradoxically, to underrate the Palestinians and hold them in contempt. The dichotomy was for them unbearable: they had to believe that they were not really causing harm. Their bitter ideological opponent Vladimir Jabotinsky was not perturbed by the clash of nationalism and therefore was more respectful. In a famous essay, "The Iron Wall," he wrote: "Peace-seekers amongst us try to convince us that the Arabs are fools, or that they can be cheated by a softened interpretation of our goals, or that they are a greedy tribe ready to give up its prerogatives in Palestine for cultural or economic benefits.

I totally reject that assessment of the Arab character. They understand not less than we what is not desirable for them." He concluded that "in Palestine, two peoples will live forever." He believed that the only way to reach an agreement would be to create an "iron wall" of Jewish military force. Until such force is created, he argued, Zionists should forgo all attempts to reach a compromise. Labor-Zionism, however, persevered even when it was clear that an agreement was unattainable. They needed the hope or the illusion to pacify their liberal-socialist conscience. Ben-Gurion, who believed wholeheartedly in the possibility of an agreement, finally despaired, admitted his mistake, and later became identified with hard-line anti-Arab policies. Despite the change, the psychological need to avoid the dichotomy persisted. A conceptual externalization of the Palestinians replaced class-struggle perceptions. The conflict became Israeli-Arab, engulfing "the region" rather than Palestine. The Palestinians vanished physically and conceptually—now to be termed infiltrators, refugees, minorities—only to "re-emerge" in 1967. This "new" Palestinian phenomenon has caused many liberal, dovish Israelis to view Israel's occupation as conforming to the Algerian model. It was as if Israel equals France, and the occupied territory beyond the "green line" equals Algeria. The West Bank had been treated as a detached entity; its settlers resembled the *pied-noir;* policies of control of Arab inhabitants and land confiscation had been viewed as novel, unrelated to the policies applied to the Israeli Arabs since 1948; the demography of the territories as well as its "national accounts" were treated separately. By creating a conceptual separation between the territories and "Metropolitan Israel," a total break from the past could be achieved, and the problem could be defined in more manageable and convenient terms. The Algerian model, on which the PLO based its strategy, gained legitimacy. For the Palestinians, though, there is no differentiating between the West Bank and the whole of Palestine. For them the model applies to Israel as a whole. When asked about Israeli dovish perceptions, they observe that there were indeed plans in Algeria to detach the French-populated coastal regions and leave the hinterland for the Arabs. If the model applies, it applies all the way. Evidence supplied on the growing integration, on the development of multifaceted interactions in all areas of human and communal activity were dismissed. Comparisons of discriminatory policies and actions vis-à-vis the Palestinians in the West Bank to pre- and post-1967 policies toward Israeli Arabs were treated as Likud propaganda.

Inconsistencies such as treating the West Bank area annexed to Jerusalem as Israel proper or recording Jewish settlers' economic activity in the West Bank as Israeli were overlooked. It was Likud who related the post-1967 period to the hundred years of Jewish-Arab strife, so Labor had to refute it and insist that 1967 was the beginning of it all. Liberal Israelis preserved the nonexistent "green line" with a religious zeal, as a psychological barrier defending their world view against reality. In *The New York Times*, Anthony Lewis, who sympathizes with liberal-socialist Israelis, expresses this psychological need: "There are no signs marking the old borders of Israel; but when you cross, it feels like another country. Few Israelis visit the West Bank now; it is an uncomfortable place. It feels indigestible." This sentiment is not shared by hundreds of thousands of Israeli and Palestinian youth who have come of age since 1967. The fact that they do not remember the "green line" or the years of partition—that for them Jordanians are as relevant as Ottomans—is considered a matter of political brainwashing. But there is a stronger device yet to maintain externalization of the conflict: the "Jordanian option." It enables Labor to express a genuine desire for peace without coming to terms with the community that had to pay for their spectacular achievements. Liberal conscience is too delicate for such cruel facts. Indeed it could have been very comfortable had King Hussein obliged. It would mean, of course, that one system of coercion replaces another, and Jordanian soldiers instead of Israelis would disperse Palestinian demonstrations. But this is not Israel's affair, she deals only with sovereign states.

King Hussein, however, doesn't oblige, and the indications are that he would never accept the areas offered to him as a fair territorial compromise. But this is irrelevant because he can always be depicted as intransigent, and anyway, there is a peace policy to be presented.

In the meantime, the internally generated conflict is raging: in terrorist acts, communal rioting, Israeli vigilantism, and land confiscation; on the garbage trucks and in Beth Shemesh. The Israeli occupation almost exceeds the Jordanian occupation in length of time, but no realistic policies are formulated. The situation has degenerated into an endemic plural (or dual) condition, and the Algerian-colonial model seems less and less applicable. The curtain falls on another act of the tragedy, soon to rise again, and the cathartic relief is late in coming.

In late 1979 I published an article in which I wrote,

The pattern created by Israeli policies and all social, economic and political community interactions assumed a quasi-permanent nature. Moreover, all indications point to the conclusion that these processes will continue without serious interruption. It is assumed that occupation is by definition temporary, and the present ties between Israel and the occupied territories will alter radically with the removal of military government and the signing of a peace treaty. However, the processes set in motion after 1967 are apparently so strong that integration has passed the point of no return. It does not mean that a secession is not possible, but that solution or any other arrangement devised to replace the present political setup will have to relate to the real social, economic and political conditions in Palestine in the eighties.

My approach had been reality-oriented rather than politically oriented. As a student and as a practitioner I followed the beginnings of Jewish suburban spillover to the West Bank and understood the powerful forces unleashed by lifting the ban on land purchase and the building of roads. I studied Jewish-Arab interactions in Jerusalem's factories, Oriental Jews' attitudes toward the Arabs, and was intrigued by the appeal of fundamentalist Gush Emunim. It all seemed to me more meaningful than the political debates on a Jordanian option, Palestinian attitudes, PLO-Hashemite quarrels, or grand diplomatic demarches.

At the time, there were fewer than fifteen thousand Israelis in the territories; it was before Likud launched its massive land alienation process, before Israeli law was applied personally to the settlers, before the establishment of civilian administration, before Begin's second term, and before the evacuation of Sinai and particularly the Lebanon war. I had no reason, five years later, to back up or to admit mistake. Indeed, the processes accelerated and the momentum became stronger. In the meantime I had opened my Zionist history books, and reevaluated my own political philosophy. I found out how firmly the present is rooted in the past, and realized the potency of old Zionist symbols and how they influence present perceptions and actions. I realized that what I had perceived as an unbridgeable ideological cleavage between my own group, Labor-Zionism, and the "other" political culture, Likud, had narrowed down to a mere difference in style. Looking back on Zionist politics, I realized that disagreement on goals of Zionism created rivalries and even enmity among Zionist factions, but the disputes masked an agreement in principle on the national objective: the establishment of an independent national entity based on a Jewish majority in the Land of Israel. All Zionist groups joined together to create concrete political, military, social, and economic realities that led to the establishment of the State of Israel and the consolidation of its strength. I followed the tragic clash of subjective will and objective reality in personalities like David Ben-Gurion and Arthur Ruppin, and reflected on how we have found ourselves controlling the whole of Western Palestine.

The realization of Zionism's maximum aims was not predestined and did not follow a planned grand design. The constraints with which Zionism had to contend, the reaction of its enemies, domestic and external political coalition, global politics—all of those led to that result. There were two consistent themes in that story: Jewish single-minded power-building and Palestinian uncompromising resistance. I reflected on the Palestinian contribution to the realization of Zionist maximum goals. At every stage in the progress of Zionism there were clear choices both for Jews and for Arabs. Zionist leadership tried to reach a compromise only to be flatly and violently rejected by the Palestinians. It happened in 1936, when the Zionists had accepted a partition that gave them a third of Mandatory Palestine, and again in 1947, when the U.N. partition offered the Palestinians half the land. From the Palestinian point of view, rejection was unavoidable. They refused to compromise because they saw Zionism as an unjust intrusion. But their subjective will had to contend also with objective realities. They underrated the Zionists and believed they could eliminate them by force of arms. It was heroic but disastrous. One recalls the remark of a French general watching the charge of the Light Brigade: "C'est magnifique, mais ce n'est pas la guerre" ("It's magnificent, but it's not war"). The Palestinians were not fighting mighty armies of a powerful empire, just militias of a community that even in 1947 they outnumbered two to one. Surely they had to realize that it was not military might that defeated them but was instead the desperate courage of a wounded animal. Admittedly they were not morally responsible for the Jewish tragedy and must have felt infinite rage at the world that made them pay for the wickedness of others. It is true that their only guilt had been that they stood in the way. Yet they had to acknowledge the desperate force behind the Zionist roller coaster for their own sake, for sheer self-preservation. Trapped, however, in the rejection of any short-term settlement if it contradicted their ultimate goal, convinced that one must not compromise on matters of principle in a just cause, the Palestinians waged a hopeless life-and-death struggle with the Zionists. They were contemptuous of the Jews until it was too late. But even then they did not cease to believe that they would succeed in exterminating Zionism by force, and thus they brought disaster upon themselves. Their uncompromising approach obliged, as we have seen, even those Zionist groups that hoped for a compromise to adopt a policy of military confrontation. The prolongation of the struggle exacerbated the elements of Zionist ideology that emphasized power at the expense of those that emphasized humanitarian concern. As military force grew, it was increasingly seen as the only solution to the problem. Thus many Israelis became mirror images of the Palestinians, and thus we found ourselves on the river Jordan.

Then political, military, and socioeconomic processes began operating toward the integration of the territories into Israel. They began hesitantly but gathered momentum as the occupation wore on. By 1983, after the Lebanon war, I ventured to conclude that the clock had struck midnight and a new phase has begun. I said: "Theoretically the process might be reversible, but a realistic estimate of the forces at work for annexation as against those that oppose it leads to the conclusion that for the foreseeable future all of Palestine will be ruled by an Israeli government; that the Israeli-Palestinian conflict has therefore become an internal ethnic conflict and that Israel is now a dual society."

Historical turning points, like birthday celebrations, are meant to put time and processes in perspective, to create artificial landmarks in the perpetual sequence of events. They should not be taken literally but rather as a method to highlight qualitative changes that occur when processes reach some theoretical critical mass. I felt that such a dramatic device was required because all those involved in the tragedy or witnessing it are captives of an obsolete paradigm and refuse to let realities penetrate their well-guarded preconceptions. It is cozy to believe that time stands still, options remain open forever, and processes are open-ended or can be reversed at will. In the particular instance of the occupied territories there was a universally accepted landmark called "annexation." This constitutional term had been perceived as a reliable and objective turning point because it negates "occupation." Most observers believed that only the formal application of Israeli law to the territories constitutes a clear sign for a fundamental change. Until that fateful move takes place, the territories remain the way they were on the day military occupation was proclaimed. Indeed, structural changes have been noticed and recorded, but they were regarded as immaterial because they affected merely the socioeconomic and psychological plane and not the political-diplomatic plane, which was the only context in which the territories were perceived.

Yet I realized that "annexation" will never occur, because the present fluid, amorphic situation suits everybody, friend and foe alike. Those who favor annexation do not need the formal act: one does not annex one's own homeland. As for the practical aspects of applying the Israeli system, a better method has been found that is particularly convenient because it effectively excludes Palestinians and does not entail dealing with the permanent status of the "local population." Military government by decree is also free from normal checks and balances, and allows the settlers to operate as an *imperium in imperio*. The opponents of annexation are interested in retaining the illusion of nonannexation because the existing military occupation indicates a *temporary* arrangement—which leads to still another illusion: that political options remain open and everything is fluid. Palestinians fear the symbolic significance of annexation. It is perceived as a death sentence, the final disappointment of their hopes. Palestinian leadership, mainly PLO, view annexation as an irreversible act that would render all their political struggle futile.

All sides are interested in data showing how far things have gone, each from his own perspective: annexationists want to prove how successful they are in attaining their goals; antiannexationists want to warn that something should be done. Yet no fundamental conclusions are allowed to be drawn from that data because it will force everybody to reconsider their conceptual framework.

There was no apparent reason to try and shatter that curious unanimity, except that I found the coziness too dangerous. I feared that the system was becoming respectable, and the ambiguity about its true character serves only one segment—those who are determined to perpetuate the status quo. The symptoms were familiar: dual administration and institutional systems, disenfranchisement of 1.3 million people, lack of basic human and communal rights, double standard in services, spatial segregation. Parallels could be drawn from the four corners of the globe, none very flattering. Yet the system was allowed to develop and become institutionalized, sheltered behind the respectable shield of military occupation. Civil libertarians and progressive Israelis criticized and indeed struggled against blatant violations of human rights, Jewish vigilantism, and expulsions but dared not repudiate the fundamental, constitutional legitimacy of the system, the arbitrary and partisan tyranny disguised as military government. Their approach was political: withdrawal, territorial compromise, peace agreement. But they could offer no realistic answers to a situation that is apparently resistant to a comprehensive solution. Theoretically there were two basic norms to choose from: international law governing belligerent occupation, specifically, the Hague and the Geneva conventions; or the Israeli Declaration of Independence and Israeli laws. One of these had to serve as the basic norm in the territories. The international norm was never applied, since most Israelis could not view the territories as enemy territories and chose to apply only the humanitarian rules contained in the international conventions. After eighteen years of Israeli rule, nothing remains of the "international law" norm. Yet the facade remained and could not be challenged because the alternative—the application of Israeli norms, and not necessarily by formal application—would "amount to annexation."

In 1983 a committee appointed by the attorney general

found strong evidence for total lack of due process of law in the territories in relation to serious acts of vandalism, firing, and harassment committed by Jewish settlers against Palestinians. When the committee's report was debated in a Knesset committee, dovish, liberal members raised the constitutional question: Is the debate proper, as dealing with the report in the Israeli legislature "might indicate annexation."

And what, I thought, if no diplomatic solution is found in ten years? What about our children who are brought up in that system with their parents telling them, "It's all right—it's only temporary"? And what is the relationship between the legitimacy we render the system and the fact that Likud and more extremist parties gain in the army and among the youth three times more votes than in the general electorate?

For many years, I argued, it had been possible to justify the system of governance as military occupation, which temporarily deprives the occupied citizens of their rights until the signing of a peace treaty. Now the "temporary" occupation merely camouflages the consolidation of a hierarchy of superiors and inferiors. It has been fashionable in Israel to raise the specter of a binational state, meaning the loss of the Jewish nation-state, by absorbing 1.3 million Palestinians. So I raised another question: Is Israel to be a Jewish state or a democratic one? Moreover, I argued that this hypothetical question had become an immediate dilemma demanding an immediate answer. Otherwise the answer will be given by default.

My conclusions confounded my own wishes. They stood against everything I believed in. They amounted to an admission of total failure to prevent a situation I and my political friends warned against. Yet I thought I should contend with the realities as I see them and warn my friends that this battle is lost and we should prepare for the next. Otherwise we will lose the whole war.

I expected strong reactions but not the outpouring of abuse from my own friends. "Premature," "spreading despair," "Likud spokesman," and "naïve" were but a few of the terms used. A Knesset faction of an important dovish party agreed to let me speak in a meeting "only if I use the opportunity to disavow my views." When in an Israeli-Palestinian dialogue held in Jerusalem somebody asked why I was not invited, he was answered that had I been present, the focus of the discussion would have shifted from a "constructive path" to nihilism.

Although the factual basis for my conclusions was not challenged, its significance was: "If roads and waterworks determined political boundaries," said one, referring to my findings on the development of Israeli infrastructure in the territories, "we would all still be part of the Roman Empire, from Scotland to Arabia." Others pointed out that the number of Jewish settlers in the territories is only thirty thousand and they amount to less than 4 percent of the Palestinian population. Still others applied to the West Bank the Sinai model: if the Jewish settlement in Sinai could be evacuated, why not in the West Bank? But the main debate evolved around the philosophical question of "irreversibility." "There is no such thing as irreversibility; everything human beings do is reversible except murder," said one. "Irreversibility is in part feeling it; reality is partly perception. So long as Israelis and Palestinians think there can be a settlement based on territorial compromise, that is a reality," argued another. Perhaps the most poignant remark was this: "Meron has a tremendous point, but the way he argues it brings too much despair. We liberals cannot say we see no alternative but a binational state. Then my son will emigrate." The painful conflict between subjective will and objective reality is expressed in the following comment: "It is simply not acceptable, as the consequences are too serious."

I dismissed the accusations of despair that implied that when one is told his real condition, one is discouraged and falls into apathy. There are two schools in medicine on telling a patient about his real condition but only one unequivocal position on the need of the diagnostician not to be carried away by wishful thinking. The reaction to painful facts is not necessarily negative. Some of the greatest liberating philosophies emerged out of despair; Zionism and socialism are but two. And anyway it is traditional to kill the messengers who bring bad tidings. Selective interpretation of reality is human. In that context the Roman Empire metaphor is pertinent. Of course roads and infrastructure did not determine boundaries; willpower and resources did, and as long as they existed, boundaries held. But infrastructure transmitted power and facilitated human life and energy, which in turn recharged power. It is not the inert objects that create historic facts but rather the life they support, which continues as long as there is a will to sustain the system. It is not by accident that many European towns trace their origin to humble Roman legionary camps. This after all had been the Zionist strategy, and it did not do too badly.

The significance of data on construction of homes and roads, on Arab labor and on settlers is not in the figures but rather in the human activity created, the diffused market demand forces unleashed, and the atavistic urges nurtured. All these combined strengthen the will to perpetuate the status quo. It is difficult to combat these forces with ideological arguments such as the specter of binationalism. Most Israelis couldn't care less what you call the system as long as it permits them to maintain their newly acquired personal prosperity. With the active moral and financial support of the government, consumerism became identified with patriotism. It is very convenient to belittle these pseudopatriotic sentiments. But they draw their strength from classical Zionist concepts that sustain the raison d'être of Israel west of the "green line" too. Reality is partly perception. But the dilemma is how much to allow one's subjective will to resist reality and what price one is willing to pay for the only irreversible or perishable commodity we possess—time. Is time working for us or against us? The lesson from the past eighteen years, during which we preached the same message, is obvious: during that period our own basic positions have been eroded, and the chance to convert more people to our philosophy shrank.

The debate reminded me of the fundamental dispute between communists and reformists that tore the socialist movement apart at the turn of the century. Communists "knew" that the revolution will ultimately come when objective power relationships would change as they are "bound" to change. According to scientific Marxism, capitalism must be destroyed by its own inner contradictions. Therefore, any attempt to improve working conditions, any attempt to cope with the malaise would perpetuate it, argued the communists. Reformists were considered traitors to the cause because they fought for an eight-hour workday. Modern Western Communist parties learned. They ask themselves what can be done in the meantime and how to influence the objective processes. Israeli liberals still believe that the objective market-demand processes can be influenced by preaching self-determination without devising policies on how to achieve that lofty goal, and in the meantime they grant legitimacy to a system deliberately set to hinder that same goal. The most revealing reaction I heard was, "I cannot permit myself to accept that a Palestinian state is not feasible, because the coalition of Israeli forces, weak as it is, which supports it, is far stronger than the one ready to fight for Palestinian civil rights in a unitary state." There was a point in this remark, for many doves support territorial compromise not because of civil-libertarian views, but because they are xenophobic. Also, one cannot appoint oneself a champion of civil rights for Palestinians who refuse to demand them lest it be construed that they despair of an independent state. When asked about such an eventuality, a Palestinian intellectual replied, "No—one still hopes that something will be done to avoid these terrible prospects." Israeli liberals and Palestinians pin their hopes on a deus ex machina—some external power that would deliver them from their predicament. All eyes are focused on the U.S. to exert pressure on Israel, or on enlightened Western public opinion —in fact on everybody except themselves. "There is no such thing as irreversibility unless you assume that a country can forever decide its own fate, which is not true even of the

United States," claimed one Israeli dove. The indications are, however, that the world is sick and tired of the perpetual tribal conflict between Jews and Arabs. External involvement in our conflict was a result of the perception of the Palestine conflict as the major cause of the endemic instability in the Middle East. It was believed also that the supply of oil to the West was linked to the solution of the Palestinian problem. But these are outdated perceptions. After the collapse of OPEC, the endemic tension in the Persian Gulf, the peace treaty with Egypt, the war in Lebanon—only a few still relate the West Bank to realpolitik. It remained as an issue almost exclusively within the circle of civil libertarians and leftist radicals, a constituency possessing very little impact on the world affairs and certainly incapable of exerting effective pressure on the Israeli government. It is indeed extremely hard to perceive the full meaning of Edward Said's statement that "the Jews of Israel will remain; the Palestinians will also remain," or to accept the "internally generated conflict" concept. It is especially difficult for people who out of noble ideological reasons had to externalize the Palestinians. For them the multifaceted nature of existing group interactions is painful because they must choose between their nationalistic "Jewish state" objective and their humanistic values on daily issues such as water and land. For many years they could maintain a real or perceived ideological equilibrium, but reality permits it no longer, and further vacillation will decide the issue by default—toward ethnocentrism and against humanism. They can be justifiably angry at the reactionary forces that tilted Zionism toward xenophobia, fundamentalism, and chauvinism. Yet they should not smash the mirror just because the collective image of which they are a part looks unbecoming.

After all, the whole argument is only about a theoretical "turning point." Everybody agrees that it is all a matter of time. In one rare public debate I was invited to participate in, I was attacked by dovish speakers for being naïve and an alarmist who had lost his nerve, and was praised by hawkish speakers. But when I began to describe the situation, the reactions reversed. At the end I lost my temper and used a gynecological metaphor: "We all know that she is pregnant. Some welcome the baby, some don't. I say she is in her seventh month; you say she is only in the third. Shouldn't we prepare for the baby anyway? I know you'll always be right, because when it comes you will say, 'You see? It came only now. That is what happens to a young unmarried girl who misses her period and pretends she lost count.' "

Likud and the settlers adopted me. They were delighted with what they wanted to read into my study—that their hold over the land is secure. In *Nekuda*, the organ of Gush Emunim, an editorial stated, "We are encouraged by Benvenisti's findings, which state that Jewish settlement is so firmly established, that its dismantling or even putting it under foreign sovereignty is inconceivable. Therefore he suggests that a plan be devised which will enable the two populations, the Jewish and the Arab, to coexist according to Israel's legal system. We give our blessing to this." Yet Likud officials, especially those who deal with foreign diplomats and press, were extremely uneasy about my statements on the dual system, the treatment of the Palestinians, and the prospects of a "horse and rider" society. Likud positive reactions reinforced my isolation because they served the "peace camp" as a proof of my desertion.

I reflected on the irony: a concerned liberal documenting the dynamics of a disastrous process finds himself rejected by his own reference group and endorsed by his adversaries. It is the case of Shibboleth: "Art thou an Ephraimite? If he said, Nay; Then said they unto him, Say now Shibboleth: and he said Sibboleth: for he could not frame to pronounce *it* right. Then they took him, and slew him . . ." (Judges 12:5–6). Shibboleth in our case is "annexation," not the legal term—which nobody knows the meaning of anyway—but the notion of staying or leaving the territories. If one concludes, regretfully, that we shall be there in the foreseeable future, but it will mean the end of Israel as we know it, all qualifications, expressions of dismay, even horror are pushed aside. He is an Ephraimite.

Yet the point I sought to make was altogether different. I defined it as an immediate dilemma, indicating a choice, and expressed an urgent plea: that a new ideological equilibrium would recreate options, including the option of partition. At present, I argued, options are foreclosed because for eighteen years actions were taken casually or deliberately to close options; they can be re-created provided that the reality of the mid-eighties and not the mid-sixties be perceived.

The dilemma is not new; it has only become more urgent. We have been faced with it ever since the seventh day of the Six-Day War. It can be defined as a choice between three basic Israeli-Zionist goals: land, state, and humanistic values. Or more specifically—*moledet*, Jewish state, and liberal democracy. All three could not live together. Keeping the territories meant losing the Jewish nation state or its liberal-democratic character. At first the dilemma did not present itself as acutely, although farsighted thinkers such as Yishayahu Leibowitz and Yitshak Ben Aharon warned that unless an immediate and unilateral withdrawal was carried out, a dynamic process would begin and would tip the scales, destroying liberal democracy and the moral fiber of our society. Israeli statesmen chose, as we have seen, to evade the issue or refused to perceive its metapolitical significance, and consequently the freedom of choice narrowed. Neo-*moledet*, neo-Zionism, and fundamentalist conceptions had transformed the relative weight of the three goals in the national ethos. Moreover, the Jewish state, with pronounced ethnocentrist emphasis, and Eretz Israel became supreme moral imperatives. As the importance of these goals was enhanced, the value of the third diminished. Sensitivity to liberal, humanistic values decreased inside Israel, and especially in the territories. The interplay of internal Israeli processes, mainly the transformed belief system, time effect, and major changes in regional and global conditions, allowed to suggest that a turning point is imminent, or already passed.

A new phase has begun in which one Zionist goal, control

over the whole of Mandatory Palestine, ceased to be a variable and became a constant. The choice remained between a Jewish state and a liberal democracy.

For my liberal friends this is an impossible choice, and therefore they want to avoid it by assuring themselves and others that the land option is still open—and realistic. But if it is so, and the fear of losing other values is that acute, surely it must manifest itself in a greater sense of urgency and in willingness to pay a fitting price—in generous territorial compromises. Unfortunately this is not the case.

It seems, however, that the outcry against the conclusion that the land option is foreclosed stems from more profound and troubling reasons. It is the unwillingness to address the problem in its most basic human meaning and the fundamental reluctance to apply concrete universal norms to the territories. Why are political or academic freedom, equalization of labor conditions, termination of discrimination in the economy, or an end to usurpation of water resources construed as signs of "annexation" and therefore in conflict with comprehensive solutions? Why does a decision to apply the same standards granted to Israeli settlers to Palestinians amount to annexation, while the initial double standard is considered a temporary expediency?

Israel insists on open borders, free movement of persons and goods, normal and friendly relations between the populations. All these can be implemented unilaterally here and now, and can serve as a basis for the future. The answer of the official responsible for Arab labor whom I quoted earlier is indicative. The problem is in abeyance "until the future of the territories is determined and the negotiating parties will decide . . ." It is all political and depends on Arab willingness to accept our terms. In the meantime we don't need to test our humanistic, liberal values against our Zionist Jewish state imperatives, because we might find ourselves wanting. I deliberately refrain from mentioning the all-purpose cover of security, which is constantly used to explain inequities; it is too easy.

The instinctive recoiling from a "binational state" also needs some probing. It is a recipe for eternal strife, as indeed has been the experience of all multiethnic polities except Switzerland. But to elevate the concept of a Jewish homogeneous nation-state to the level of supreme moral imperative plays only into the hands of those who would sacrifice other values to safeguard it. What if despite all efforts we find ourselves in a quasi-permanent situation of a multiethnic polity? Would we really pack and leave, like my friend's warning about his son, or would we rather be obliged by our humanistic-liberal conviction to create consociational arrangements such as cantonization, power-sharing, and other devices that would reconcile conflicting imperatives? The reaction I quoted earlier on the weakness of Israeli forces that can be mobilized to struggle for civil rights in a unitary polity is even more defeatist than my "irreversibility" thesis. I do not argue that binationalism is the only alternative—and certainly not a preferred one—but as an unwelcomed consequence it should be studied, not contemptuously dismissed as heresy just because it is unpleasant. The founding fathers were faced with an equal dilemma: the territory of the Jewish state as drawn by the U.N. in 1947 contained an Arab population that amounted to 49 percent of the total. The Jewish leadership did not shrink from that eventuality, but accepted it and offered assurances to the U.N. In a memorandum they submitted they stated: "What will be the character of the state? It will be an independent self-governing Palestinian state with a Jewish majority, in which all citizens, regardless of race or creed, will enjoy equal rights, and all communities will control their internal affairs. The state will not be Jewish in the sense that its Jewish citizens will have more rights than their non-Jewish fellows or that the Jewish community will be superior in status to other communities, or that other religions will have an inferior rank to the Jewish religion." The Israeli Declaration of Independence was formulated before the scale of Arab exodus was known, and it addressed itself to a multiethnic situation. Indeed the Arab exodus eliminated the complication and simplified matters, but those who had assured the U.N. had not known that. Some of them are still active in Israeli politics and especially active in the peace camp. Why was it then kosher to prepare for the eventuality and it is tref (nonkosher) now? If partition is affected, it might again prove theoretical. But to ponder the question is important because it tests fundamental ideological positions.

For Likud all this is not theoretical. As they rule out partition, they assume a multiethnic polity. For them it is a concrete dilemma, and they cannot hide behind temporariness. Are they ready to repeat the assurances of 1947? From their statements one can draw the conclusion that liberal democracy is sacrificed on the altar of a Jewish state. Their perception of the Israeli polity is of a *Herrenvolk democracy* where the minority is disenfranchised and deprived of basic civil rights. In contrast, the majority enjoys all the attributes of democracy. This repressive regime is justified by neo-Zionist philosophy that emphasizes a superior moral Jewish claim. The unattractive, reactionary contradiction between Jewish state and democracy is masked by the formula that Israeli citizenship will be extended to all Palestinians who would ask for it and declare allegiance to Zionist goals or by suggesting that Palestinians would exercise their political rights in Jordan—two preposterous propositions.

The Israeli body politic, like all multiethnic entities, is faced with three, simple-to-define alternatives: majority tyranny, power-sharing, or partition. The present situation corresponds to the first alternative, although it is disguised as a temporary arrangement. Partition or power-sharing both need the agreement of two parties. The partition of Palestine, established de facto in 1948, created at tremendous human and material cost two almost homogeneous areas that could have become a long-term solution to the conflict. Since then, however, the two national groups have become entangled in multilevel quasi-permanent interaction and are interspersed territorially. Partition would require not only a fundamental change in political perceptions but again as in 1948, tremendous human and material costs. Considering the alternatives, however, it seems the only long-term solution. Power-sharing or consociational arrangements require a minimum of willingness of the elite to cooperate across the sectarian divide. It cannot be instituted against the wishes of the majority segment, let alone against the wishes of both segments. Therefore, "living together peacefully" does not seem a realistic possibility but rather a recipe for eternal strife and instability.

As both alternatives to the present political structure are either impractical in the short run or unattractive in the long run, the existing—and worst—alternative prevails and becomes pervasive. There is no escape, and short-term alternatives must be found to combat the institutionalization of a *Herrenvolk* democracy.

In this, attitudes and actions of the Palestinians are crucial. Whereas the Israeli predicament is conceptual and ideological, Palestinian suffering is real. For them the present situation is unbearable and must alter drastically. Yet many of them believe that because it must change, it will. They feel that only one solution, based on their national objective of establishing a state of their own, is feasible. In the long run it is indeed the only long-term solution, but the problem is that they are powerless to attain it. They find themselves caught in the apparent contradiction between short-term action, which under the circumstances means operating within the realm of the possible under Israeli rule, and the long-term, comprehensive objective of self-determination. Operating within the system is construed as legitimizing the status quo. In that, their dilemma is similar to that of Israeli liberals, and they suffer the same consequences—inability to devise realistic policies, which in turn license the continuation of the status quo. Yet the key is held by the Palestinians. As the suffering party on whose behalf Israeli liberals struggle, only they can legitimize short-term action. Without their sanctioning, Israeli liberals are paralyzed. Palestinian freedom of action is objectively limited by Israeli control, but they are not powerless. One wrong conclusion drawn from the present phase in the Israeli-Palestinian conflict is that the Palestinians are utterly beaten and incapable of affecting their own future. The destruction in 1982 of their semiindependent state in Lebanon set the Palestinian people back twenty years. Once again, for the third time (after 1948 and 1967), they turned into a flock of refugees subject to the mastery of the states that give them asylum, serving as pawns in their hands. Once again the strategy of armed struggle against the Zionists failed, and with it another misconception, that of *al-kharej* (the outside). It was PLO belief, sustained by diplomatic and political successes, that external action would influence *al-dakhel* (the inside), the occupied territories. Intoxicated by victories such as Yassir Arafat's U.N. speech in 1974, they were encouraged to think that political gains, combined with terrorism, would effectively defeat Israel.

They refused, just like Israeli liberals, to understand the significance of the physical facts created in the territories, and that the point of no return is approaching. The Palestinian population in the territories has been subdued, because both Israel and the PLO have joined forces to destroy any chance for the growth of local political leadership. The radical leadership torpedoes every attempt to adopt realistic policies, and those who preached for short-term action to resist annexation were stigmatized as traitors, or assassinated.

The Palestinians, however, possess an enormous asset—the basic fact that two million of them stayed on their land. Despite Israeli discriminatory policies they have prospered enormously, and their natural population growth continues to be very high. More significantly, they have managed to resist attempts of the Israelis to fragment them. Their communal cohesion remains strong, and a younger generation, better educated and dedicated, is beginning to replace the older elite. Israeli political thinking underestimates the internal Palestinian factor. PLO political maneuvering and Israeli security-oriented perceptions overshadow the slow but steady accumulation of internal Palestinian communal power. Its true potential will be realized only when Palestinians decide to move in the system. As long as their activity is expressed in violence and rejection, it can be dismissed as a problem of control. Once they adopt Zionist tactics—a balanced policy of communal power-building—the Israeli predicament would cease to be theoretical. Short-term objectives do not necessarily preclude options for long-term solutions. In fact constructivist Zionism defined only intermediate, achievable goals. The long-term goal was implied in the self-identification as a national liberation movement. Zionism identified unchangeable elements that affected the short-term and did not stand in any essential contradiction to long-term arrangements. Serving in the British security forces could be construed as treason but also as another conquest that slowly builds up a power base. That tactic proved successful and more productive in the long run than Jewish terrorist activity,—despite recent attempts to rewrite Zionist history. Once Palestinians adopt such policies, Israeli liberals would find it easier to join hands with them. It is true that few Israelis are ready to give up their Jewish state, but many Israelis perceive the Palestinian predicament in humanitarian rather than political terms. They oppose a Palestinian state but are ashamed of mistreatment and vigilantism, and are ready to fight for short-term goals.

The reader who has patiently followed my meandering narrative has probably detected many inconsistencies that I cannot explain. But one I can—and want to—clarify. When describing the Jerusalem environment, I criticized the open-ended, process-oriented approach and assumed a principled, solution-oriented posture. On the West Bank, however, I advocate the opposite and criticize the solution-oriented approach. This seeming inconsistency is the result of the contradiction inherent in Israeli perceptions of the two environments. Jerusalem is perceived as an internal Israeli issue because it was legally and conceptually detached from the West Bank and turned into another Israeli city, like Natanya.

To perceive it in the macropolitical context is inconvenient because it raises delicate problems. Therefore it is depicted as a social, microethnic matter. The West Bank, however, is treated only as an external issue. To treat it other than as a macropolitical problem is inconvenient because it implies permanency, or to use the shibboleth, "annexation." The different conceptual treatment of Jerusalem and the West Bank shows again how problems are defined by the cozy solution and not vice versa.

As a compulsive *advocatus diaboli*, I sought to highlight the missing element in both perceptions and hence the inconsistency. If one treats both environments as equal, as one should, my approach is consistent. In endemic situations the pragmatic, symptomatic approach is more appropriate provided it rests on firm, immutable humanistic principles. The admirable but useless massive political engineering is heroic and principled; modest, incremental changes, however, seem to work better in endemic situations. Raja Shehadeh, in his book *The Third Way*, describes the new bitter but realistic Palestinian interim goal emerging from their protracted suffering: to steadfastly cling to the land, to work the system with dignity and perseverance, and not to fall into the terrorist or the collaborator trap. It is a personal, moving document, not a political program. But such a program is bound to be formulated. It is only a matter of time. Shehadeh was encouraged by Israeli response, although he confused humanitarian sympathy with political support. But humanitarian sympathy is a powerful instrument for combatting inequalities and may help to build a viable bridge over the sectarian divide that ultimately could create political options.

There is a strong element of *moledet* in Raja Shehadeh's book. He is standing on a hilltop, watching the golden strip of the Mediterranean coastline, yearning for Jaffa, his parents' native city, now assimilated in Tel Aviv; his best Jewish friend is a *moledet* enthusiast; he laments the destruction of the environment by brutal Israeli bulldozers cutting through the terraced olive groves. A mirror image of our *moledet*. Reading Shehadeh's moving narrative, I remembered what an Arab friend had said when I pointed out the relative scarcity of Arab literary expressions of longing for the homeland when compared with Jewish expressions: "A man who lives with his beloved," he replied, "feels no need to give poetic expressions to his feelings, for she is tangible. Only he who has lost his beloved, is far away from her, or unsure of her love, is forced to give poetic expressions to his yearning. If, heaven forbid, we are fated to undergo two thousand years of exile, we too will write poems full of yearning for Jerusalem no less profound than yours." It took the Arabs less than two millennia.

Sumud and *moledet*, steadfastness and possession; *al-Awda* and *hashiva*—the return to Jaffa and to Bethel—the same longings, the same attachment, the same human feelings. It is hard to perceive the symmetry, for longing nurtures exclusive possessiveness, and suffering, a sense of absolute truth. Yet understanding the other's fears, hopes, and longings should not detract from one's own. Understanding is not identical with agreement. We have been at each other's throat long enough to realize each other's sincerity, no matter how long the struggle continues.

The curtain is raised on a new act of the old tragedy. Unlike earlier acts, it is supported almost exclusively by the two tragic heroes. All supporting actors have withdrawn; in center stage the two heroes conduct a dialogue. The tired audience listens to the exchange and wonders if the tragedy is close to its catharsis—or whether an even more horrifying act must be endured.

Not long ago I was invited to dinner with a Palestinian at a friend's home in an American city. As we were talking, I mentioned the name of a Jerusalem scholar, Faysal al-Husseini. "Which Husseini is he?" asked the Palestinian. "The son of 'Abd al-Qader," I replied. He looked at me and I felt the bond and break between us. The father's name was a cue. He was the charismatic military leader of the Palestinians during the 1948 war, killed on the hill of Qastal. The hill changed hands twice in close and cruel combat, and is cherished in the national myths of both Israelis and Palestinians. The host, sensing the sudden tension, asked, "And who is 'Abd al-Qader?" "He knows and I know," replied the Palestinian. Our shared homeland and native city, which the Palestinian had not visited for a generation, came up again and again; each time this strange kinship of enemies, sharing so much and yet so divided, grew. Finally, our host, an expert on Middle Eastern affairs, concluded, "Listening to you two, I vow I'll never write another line on your conflict. I don't know anything about it."

Epilogue:
What's in a Name?

A little while ago, just before the Passover vacation, my son Yuval came home with the itinerary for his school outing. My father, who was there at the time, asked to see it. Glancing through it, I could see something was making him angry. "Why are all the place names in Arabic?" he demanded. "Don't they know in the Scouts that these places have Hebrew names?" His reaction was not surprising. My father, eighty-seven, a teacher and a geographer, has devoted his whole life to one thing: creating a new Hebrew map of Eretz Israel and instilling in young people a love of country. For years he has been a member of the official "naming committees" whose task it was to Hebraize all the names on the ordnance map of Eretz Israel and to name new Jewish settlements. His maps can be seen on the walls of classrooms throughout Israel. In fact the huge blue-brown-and-green wall map he drew is imprinted in the visual memory of hundreds of thousands of Israelis.

I grew up among maps: ancient maps depicting a legendary *Terra Promissionis* drawn in Amsterdam and Hanover in the sixteenth century; maps of Napoleon's invasion in 1799; maps of European explorers of the nineteenth century; aerial photos of the German Flying Corps in the First World War; Jewish National Fund maps—all neatly stacked in drawers in my father's study. In long and boring meetings, instead of doodling absentmindedly, I draw maps of Crusader Palestine.

191

When I can't sleep I do not count sheep, I imagine myself flying over Israel, and I visualize the landscape from Eilat to Dan, every wadi, village, and mountain. Usually I fall asleep above Mount Tabor.

My father's map-making is not his craft; it is for him an act of faith. It expresses his relationship to the land, to the Jewish people and its history. "What's in a name?" asked Shakespeare. A name creates order in the world. The immediate response of Adam, the first man, to the creation of wildlife was: "And he gave them names." Coming to a new country is in a way like the Creation, and your first impulse is to impose on the new landscape some sort of order. You cannot take in huge, undifferentiated areas. How can you comprehend them? You delineate them in miniature. Any explorer has to map the terra incognita, to make it viable, organized. Map drawing and naming of physical features is an act of possession, of creating a new reality. We are not the Creator that we can create or alter physical reality, but we can organize a new grid of reference and by that we believe that we have "re-created" the country and gained symbolic ownership. Human beings cannot be forced to change their names, their self-identification, but mountains and rivers cannot complain about having their names altered.

Jorge Borges quotes an old Spanish book: "In that Empire the art of map drawing has attained such perfection that the map of one district was the size of a whole city, and the map of the whole Empire was the size of a whole district. Eventually these huge maps were not sufficient, and committees of map-drawers began to prepare the map of the Empire in the exact scale of the Empire itself, and this map was identical with the actual Empire in every point." Eventually the map was slowly destroyed by the elements: "In the Western deserts some ruins of the map survived, and wild animals and beggars reside in them." The empire could not be perceived until it was reproduced on paper. Eventually the map assumed more reality than reality itself. Maps are more manageable because they can be altered, names can be changed, there are no longer any physical constraints. There is also much more of a commitment involved in making a map than in verbal description and much more finality in naming. In describing a river I can employ all manner of subtleties. Although the river ebbs and flows, I fix it on a map for all time, unambiguously. In naming the river I give it final identity. After you have done that, you forget the reality that the map was intended to represent and you relate only to the representation. Map-makers forget that their productions are merely approximations, they begin to believe in the ultimate truth of their representation. The ambiguity and hesitancies of the draftsmen are forgotten. There is a mesmerism in maps and names.

All immigrant societies drew maps and renamed places, because then the geography became their own. They tamed the landscape with names in their own language that had significance for them: London, York, Plymouth, Perth, Amsterdam, Orleans. Succeeding generations take these names for granted.

The highest mountain in Israel is Mount Meron. Its name was Mount Jermaq. The Kabbalists of Safed knew it by its old name. But Jermaq is an Arab name, and the committees decided that the highest mountain in the country simply could not have an Arab name. They had to think of a new name, so they took the name of the village in the foothills (after which, incidentally, I am called Meron), and called it Mount Meron. Now everyone believes that it always has been Mount Meron, though its history as such does not exceed thirty years.

Map drawing is a natural impulse of people coming to a new place; the people who have lived in the country for centuries rarely need it themselves. They know their land; for them it is not a chaotic collection of mountains and ravines. They know what is beyond the horizon without consulting a map and a compass.

I remember how, during hikes in the desert, I sometimes used to hide behind a rock to consult my map. I didn't like to let on to the youth group I was guiding that I needed a piece of paper to reorient myself. Place names in the language of indigenous people are not symbolic; they are purely descriptive or even accidental. In his play *Translations*, Brian Friel describes the clash between the suspicious Irish peasantry and a British army surveyor team that comes to draft a new map of Ireland. The British needed accurate translations and "pronounceable" names, and the Irish could not comprehend the purpose of it all. What the British wanted was to delineate areas and boundaries for purposes of taxation. The project was presented to the peasantry as proof of the government's good intentions, as an attempt to bring about efficient administration.

Changing place names in order to arrive at a Hebrew map of Eretz Israel was considered by my father a sacred task. He was one of Israel's first geographers—awarded the Israel Prize for his life's work. And now, after sixty years, that his own grandson should come to him with Arab names instead of Hebrew ones seemed to him tantamount to sacrilege. Like all immigrant societies, we attempted to erase all alien names, but here the analogy becomes complicated because we were not simply an immigrant society or an army of conquerors. At our coming, we reestablished contact with those same landscapes and places from which we had been physically removed for two thousand years but whose names we had always preserved. We carried around with us for centuries our *geographia sacra*, not only biblical names but all the mishnaic and talmudic names. Wherever we were dispersed— in France, Germany, Egypt, Persia—we would study texts and learn about the rosters of priestly duty in the Temple enumerating by turn their home villages in the Galilee. People who knew nothing about the physical reality of those villages knew their names by heart. So when we returned to the land it was the most natural thing to seek out those ancient places and identify them.

Every time people traveled to Eretz Israel, there was an attempt at identification. Inevitably they made mistakes. For example, it was thought that Acre was the Philistine city of Ekron, so a nearby tower in the sea was called the Tower of Flies because the Philistines had a temple of Baalzebub—Lord of the Flies—in Ekron. The travelers manufactured an esoteric geography of Palestine, hopelessly inaccurate.

It was an American scholar, Edward Robinson, who in the mid-nineteenth century created order out of all this. He came to the conclusion that the best way to identify biblical names was to read the Bible in conjunction with Arabic place names. In one relatively short visit he conclusively identified hundreds of biblical names. His works are the basis of many of the places we have renamed. Paradoxically enough, the skeleton of the Hebrew map of Israel was immortalized and preserved by that same people whose own place names we sought to erase. This is where we differed from the English in Ireland. It was a matter of indifference to the English which sites they renamed or how place names became distorted in the process. In the Roman and later in the Crusader period, the conquerors of Palestine imposed an entirely new map on the Holy Land. The Crusader map, for example, resembled nothing more than an extension of southern France. Names like Mirabel, Château-Pelerin, Belvoir, and Montfort were Provençal transplants. Nothing remains of all that. The indigenous people scarcely adopted a single name as their own. Beth She'an was called Scythopolis for five centuries. The moment the last Roman administrator left, the place-name reverted back to Beth She'an (Beisan). The names of places established by the conquerors, like Nablus (Neapolis) or Caesarea, were adopted. The others were not preserved in local usage. The Semitic population, of which a large proportion is doubtless of the same stock as ourselves, who were Christianized and later Islamized preserved in their language our own Semitic place names without which we would never have been able to reconstruct our Hebrew map. There is a certain amount of ingratitude in that process. Because what in fact did we do? We changed the names systematically, not only those that had an ancient Hebrew name, but *all* the Arabic nomenclature including places that had only Arabic names. It was an attempt to eradicate the history of Arab Palestine—to symbolically eradicate two thousand years of our own absence from Eretz Israel.

Consider the case of Jerusalem. In 1967, after the occupation of the Old City, the government insisted upon the use of the name Urshalim in Arab-language broadcasting. This name was never used in Arabic; the city was always known as al-Quds ("the Holy"). At the time I was administrator of the Old City, I made a tacit agreement with the Israeli broadcasting authority that we use the traditional name, and one morning the radio began its broadcast in Arabic with the announcement: *"Saut Israil min al-Quds"* ("The Voice of Israel from al-Quds"). This caused a furor that reached the cabinet. I insisted on knowing why they wanted to force the Arabs to call a city holy to them by a fabrication, a Hebrew name transmogrified into Arabic. The answer was that the use of Urshalim established a political fact: Jewish rule in Jerusalem. Eventually a compromise was reached. The name would be hyphenated and the city would be known officially in Arabic as Urshalim–al-Quds. And so it has remained.

Our new map-making is different from the Crusader and the Roman periods. We are not conquerors who have fabricated a map for military and judicial purposes. We are a people that has returned and become indigenous. As long as Jews live here, speak Hebrew, and repeat these names to their children, these are the names that there will be.

We have done more than create a paper empire. We have actually transformed the physical reality, built cities, drained marshes, made the desert bloom. We not only eradicated Arab place names, we actually destroyed the places as well.

When the first Jewish geographers like my father began their work, they used the maps of Palestine that the British drew up in the 1880s. Not satisfied with their accuracy, they went out to the country accompanied by Arab dragomans who would point out and identify landmarks. Very often names were invented by guides where no specific name existed, and in time these names were immortalized. I recall a place in the Negev desert whose name on the map when translated from the Arabic would mean something like "the place where the monkeys mate." Why? Probably because the surveyor demanded a name for some rock formation that in his opinion seemed worthy of a name. The guide, probably losing patience with the whole endeavor, obliged with the first thing that came into his head. The invention was duly and solemnly recorded.

From a very early age, perhaps four or five, I and my brother would accompany my father on his Sabbath expeditions. And so it was that the Arab names of villages and mountains, groves and springs became those of my childhood. I remember the names perfectly—they became second nature to me—and when I travel around the country I unfailingly recall the previous names. The Arab names. I have a friend who lives in a Jewish village in the Jerusalem corridor. When he mentions the Hebrew name Shoevah, I immediately think of it as Saris, the Arab name.

After the war in 1967 I went to a refugee camp near Jerusalem to study and report on the needs of the refugees. I asked the people I met where they came from before the war of 1948. One told me he was from Khirbet al-Loze, one from Deir a-Sheikh, one from Ajjur . . . and I suddenly saw before my eyes that other geography—the geography of my youth. The areas where I had so often accompanied my father on his map-making travels. And I had the feeling that the men talking to me were my brothers—a feeling of sharing, affinity. Later I was to feel this same kinship between enemies, but in other contexts. I feared what would happen to these men if they were ever to go back and see that all they remembered no longer existed. I could not share in their sense of loss, but I could and did share a deep nostalgia, mixed with pain, for the landscapes of my youth. The feelings are quite unrelated to any political significance. It is not a question of whether the

1948 war was avoidable or not, or why the refugees fled, or if we had the right to dispossess them. I am speaking entirely on the emotional plane. I understand them and can share some of their pain. I can understand; I do not have to agree.

The Hebrew map of Israel constitutes one stratum in my consciousness, underlaid by another stratum of the previous Arab map. Those names turn me and anyone who was born into them into sons of the same homeland—but also into mortal enemies. I can't help but reflect on the irony that my father, by taking me on his trips and hoping to instill in me the love of our Hebrew homeland, and imprinted in my memory, along with the new names, the names he wished to eradicate.

This brings me, strangely enough, to the Lebanon war. I was aware for quite some time that Palestinian research institutes in Beirut were compiling files on each Palestinian village in Israel. Since the beginning of the war I wondered about the fate of those files. I was fairly sure that General Sharon and General Eitan would search them out, seize them, and destroy them in order to complete the eradication of Arab Palestine. This is what eventually happened when the Israeli Army entered West Beirut. I knew that some of the information in those files was purely imaginary and was used as propaganda against my country. Every refugee, even the lowliest, is convinced that he used to own at least a hundred acres of orchards and a large house in Israel. It is an understandable tendency to magnify the scale of what they lost. But the point is—and there lies the irony and the tragedy—that they have created their own *geographia sacra*, just as we did in our Diaspora. Their map-making is the answer to our Hebrew, Israeli map. They are trying by an act of will to recreate and preserve the old reality, the one we erased in order to create our own. Their map-making is as far removed from reality as our memorizing the list of villages of the priestly roster.

Not only are the refugee camps organized by sections according to the villages in Palestine from which the refugees originated, their children are taught exclusively with reference to the pre-1948 map of Palestine. On their maps hundreds of Palestinian villages, long since destroyed, are shown, but the Jewish cities, settlements, roads, and ports are omitted. Everything that happened subsequent to their departure is perceived as an aberration. Their refusal to cope with the stark and cruel reality causes them to believe that what the Jews print on their maps is sheer fiction. Some time ago I took an Arab friend to Tel Aviv. It was his first visit. Driving along the promenade, flanked by huge tourist hotels, and watching the people on the crowded beach, he said, "You know, instead of waging wars against us, you should have forced the Arab leaders to spend a weekend in one of these hotels. Then they would have understood that all this is real and that it is here to stay."

At this point in our conflict, maps cease being geographical and turn into an act of faith, a call for action, for revenge. I'll destroy your map as you have destroyed mine. A zero-sum game that is played out not only in words and symbols, but in concrete deeds of destruction.

There is no point in asking who started. It is true that my father had started his Hebrew map to gain symbolic possession of his ancestral land. But he believed that he was doing so peaceably, not disinheriting anybody. Indeed he and most of his generation genuinely believed that there was enough room in the country for everybody. The Palestinians did not take him seriously. For them he was a romantic Westerner, just like the British and German explorers who came before him and left, with their strange compasses, sextants, and theodolites. They did not realize that his map-making was of a different sort, that he intended to settle down and teach his children the names he invented, and by so doing, to perpetuate them and thus transform symbolic possession into actual possession. When the Arabs realized the danger, it was too late. They tried to destroy my father physically, but they failed. He offered them compromises, but they rejected them. Finally an all-out war decided the issue; they were driven out, and his map triumphed. Then we set out to transform the land, to construct our own edifices, to plan our own orchards. But we also deliberately destroyed the remnants our enemies left lest they come back and attempt to lay claim to it. We knew that had they won they would have destroyed our work. But we won, so we became the destroyers. Who is the victim? Who is the culprit? Who is the judge?

One of the places that still festers in my consciousness is the Peace Forest, otherwise known as Park Canada, in the foothills of the Shephela near Latrun. It was created in the early 1970s on the ruins of three Arab villages: Yalu, Beit Nuba, and 'Imwas. Their inhabitants were expelled in 1967 after the end of the hostilities, and the villages were subsequently razed to the ground. Three villages. They lay in the Latrun salient, and for strategic reasons we resolved at the time that no testimony to the existence of the villages would be left to nurture the illusion that the inhabitants would ever be allowed to return. It is irrelevant for the moment whether this consideration was justified. But to call it a Peace Forest, to take well-meaning donors and with their money turn all these orchards from which people had once earned their livelihood into a picnic area for Israelis and tourists, is something else entirely. This betrays not only a total lack of sensitivity but something that must eventually corrupt our youth. It is one thing to destroy a village in the heat of battle. Even then, your humanitarian instincts are severely tested. But war is a situation devoid of human values, our soldiers who had to go through with it were spiritually torn asunder as a result. There are moving testimonies to this in the 1948 and 1967 wars and again recently in the Lebanon war. But to undertake a deliberate policy of eradicating villages because of the well-founded fear that the other side would do the same to us—and then callously to name the area the Peace Forest—must have profound consequences for our own sense of values and those of future generations. This is not what my father had in mind when he began his innocent, romantic map-making. He may have been too naïve or too well-meaning to understand the brutal forces that were unleashed as a result of his search for his biblical roots. This does not absolve him from a share in the responsibility for what came to pass. But his adversaries, equally naïve or contemptuous of him, thought they could frighten him away so that his sons would not become indigenous to this land. They paid for their contempt and cruelty and were driven out. They share not only the responsibility for their predicament, they also share the responsibility for making us cruel. Dehumanization is a contagious disease.

Yet there is an additional element of irony in the tragedy. We can never escape the inherent struggle between our symbolic attempt to create authentically Israeli forms and the perpetual slide toward the physical forms of the Palestinians, perhaps, in a way, because we sense that they are an inalienable part of the land. Take the Tower of David, the best-known symbol of Jerusalem. Its form is simply and solely that of a minaret, and whatever you do, you cannot alter the fact that it is an Islamic, Arab structure. The ruins of the Arab villages —a few layers of weathered stone, a half-buried arch, a broken millstone—betray the previous existence of a once living, breathing village. Even where, literally, one stone does not remain upon another, you can still detect the ghost of a village. There are plants such as dill that grow only in places inhabited by men and his domestic beasts. There are *"bustans,"* groves of vine, fig, and pomegranate; there are dense hedges of sabra-cactus fencing off one property from another. Even where the village itself has completely vanished you can still discern its contours. Almost two million Palestinians still live on their land, cherish it, and are determined to preserve their own map and physical forms. It is impossible to erase their contribution to the landscape of our shared homeland, no matter how hard people try. Someone, someday, will raise the question and will demand an answer. Are we ready to merge the two maps? Are we ready to stop eradicating each other's names? When such questions can be asked, perhaps the dissonance and conflict that plague so many Israelis will be resolved.

When at a certain stage I left my own immediate surroundings to seek out a more universal dimension to my experiences, I found myself in the Grand Opera House of Belfast. The first performance of Brian Friel's *Translations* was given in the Opera House—rebuilt after twenty-four bombing incidents—to an all-Catholic audience. The play dealt with the substitution of an English map of Ireland for the original, the ultimate symbolic expression of possession. When the play ended, I said to my friend, a Catholic, "You know what? We've been doing the same thing all along—translating, changing names, creating a new reality." My friend regarded me for a moment with an expression of the utmost sadness and said at last, "Well, if that's the case, may God have mercy on you all!"

Index

ABOUT THE AUTHOR

MERON BENVENISTI is an historian and a former deputy mayor of Jerusalem. He left city government after a break with Mayor Teddy Kollek, and has since devoted himself to study of the Palestinian-Israeli relationship. He is the author of several books, has lectured widely in United States, and has written articles for *The New York Review of Books* and *The New York Times*. He lives in Jerusalem with his wife and children, on the border between an Arab and an Israeli neighborhood.